Prophesying
Tragedy

Prophesying Tragedy

SIGN AND VOICE IN SOPHOCLES' THEBAN PLAYS

Rebecca W. Bushnell

Cornell University Press

ITHACA AND LONDON

CORNELL UNIVERSITY PRESS GRATEFULLY ACKNOWLEDGES
A GRANT FROM THE ANDREW W. MELLON FOUNDATION
THAT AIDED IN BRINGING THIS BOOK TO PUBLICATION.

First published 1988 by Cornell University Press.

International Standard Book Number 0-8014-2132-2
Library of Congress Catalog Card Number 87-47857

Printed in the United States of America

*Librarians: Library of Congress cataloging information
appears on the last page of the book.*

*The paper in this book is acid-free and meets the guidelines for
permanence and durability of the Committee on Production Guidelines
for Book Longevity of the Council on Library Resources.*

To *my father,*
Douglas F. Bushnell

τῷ μὲν θεῷ καλὰ πάντα καὶ ἀγαθὰ καὶ
δίκαια, ἄνθρωποι δὲ ἃ μὲν ἄδικα
ὑπειλήφασιν ἃ δὲ δίκαια.

To a god, all things are beautiful, good,
and right; men, however, deem some things
right and others wrong.

Heraclitus 102 (Diels)

Contents

Preface

No student of tragedy should wonder that Milton assigned the topic of fate and free will to a group—or seminar—of demons in Pandemonium. Their lot was intellectual torment when they "sat on a Hill retir'd / In thoughts more elevate, and reason'd high / Of Providence, Foreknowledge, Will and Fate, / Fixt Fate, Free will, Foreknowledge absolute, / And found no end, in wand'ring mazes lost."[1] The very monotony and repetitiveness of these lines suggest that in such disputes scholars tend to go around in circles, from "fixt fate" to free will and back. Neither we nor the devils hold the thread to find the way out of the maze.

While attempting to construct a relationship between tragic characters and their "fate," students of tragedy have often turned to philosophy, only to find that the philosophers use epic, tragic, or mythical examples to support their arguments. When Plato wants to describe the nature of *anankē* ("necessity") in the *Republic*, he uses the myth of Er, picturing the Fates as turning Necessity's spindle, while legendary and epic heroes choose the lots of their lives to come. In the disputes

1. *Paradise Lost* 2:557–61, in John Milton, *Complete Poems and Major Prose*, ed. Merritt Y. Hughes (Indianapolis: Bobbs-Merrill, 1957).

between the Stoic philosophers and their critics, Oedipus's story serves as the commonplace illustration of the use of divination in a predestined world.[2] Similarly, the advocates for and against divination in Cicero's dialogue *De divinatione* draw on Homer and tragedy as well as on recent events in Roman history to construct their arguments about fate.[3]

Greek histories, too, often mix "literary" stories and logic with "historical" events. Most notably, Herodotus reports numerous examples of omens fulfilled and of the Delphic Oracle's astounding successes in predicting human events, although most of these omens and spectacular responses are probably the stuff of legend or invention.[4] Yet students of tragedy should not take Herodotus's history as simply the referent for tragedy. His history concerns us because he and the tragic playwrights shared a habit of thought, an imagination that saw human events in terms of tragic causality and "plot."

While early histories and plays mark human events as "fated" or "plotted," they also display a fascination with prophecy, the language of fate. Oracles and omens mark the outlines of the tragic plot, which is shaped by myth or history. Most modern discussions of tragedy take prophecy for granted, as a fact of nature or an important religious belief. At the same time, we assume that the tragic hero will defy the prophet who predicts disaster for him. We are expected to perform a paradox: to honor both the prophet and the hero, even as they oppose each other. Because heroes must defy prophecy and prophecy must always come true, tragedy both valorizes and criticizes opposition to authority and divinity. Oedipus, in his abuse of Tiresias and his celebration of secular values, sym-

---

2. See William Chase Greene, *Moira: Fate, Good, and Evil in Greek Thought* (Cambridge: Harvard University Press, 1944), pp. 347, 365, 376.

3. See, e.g., *De divinatione* i.72, ii.63.

4. See Joseph Fontenrose, *The Delphic Oracle: Its Responses and Operations with a Catalogue of Responses* (Berkeley: University of California Press, 1978); Roland Crahay, *La Littérature oraculaire chez Hérodote* (Paris: Belles Lettres, 1956).

bolizes everything Athenian society stood for, and yet Oedipus must fail because he threatens the sacred order prophecy represents. The hero, even when he is presented as the city's leader and a defender of its values in his defiance of prophecy, seems to come inevitably into conflict with the city's interests.

A better understanding of this situation comes from Greek history, especially as it is recounted by Thucydides, who tells how people can appropriate prophecy's authority to make a political course of action appear fated. The desire for that power is implicit in every scene of conflict between hero and prophet in tragedy's version of political life; the tragic hero is fighting not only for control over his own life but also for the right to speak for his city or country.

Thus an understanding of the relationship between humans and their epic or tragic fates can be found not in metaphysics but in history and culture, which determine a play's themes and values.[5] More specifically, the Greek tragic hero's relationship with prophecy was inseparable from political uses of prophecy: the interpretation and defiance of tragic prophecy both reflected and influenced political behavior. In its representation of prophecy, tragedy sets forth concretely the Athenians' concern with authority and freedom, while also presenting an influential model of "heroic" behavior in a political context. This model calls for both the defiance of authority and the appropriation of that authority in the city or state, through the power of interpretation.

This book examines the political dimensions of the conflict between hero and prophet in Greek tragedy, and in Sophocles' Theban plays in particular. Again and again in tragedy and epic we find characters confronting prophecy in scenes that define tragic fate. I begin with the hero's response to prophecy

---

5. As Jean-Pierre Vernant says, through tragedy the Greek city "turned itself into a theatre. Its subject, in a sense, was itself and it acted itself out before its public." See Jean-Pierre Vernant and Pierre Vidal-Naquet, *Tragedy and Myth in Ancient Greece*, trans. Janet Lloyd (Atlantic Highlands, N.J.: Humanities Press, 1981), p. 9.

in the *Iliad*'s "tragedy of Hector,"[6] the first scene of the defiance of prophecy in Western literature. Some scholars might argue that the generic difference between epic and Attic drama precludes our calling the story of Hector a "tragedy." But Hector's story, from his defiance of Polydamas's prophecy to his dying words foretelling Achilles' death, establishes the pattern of the defiance of prophecy: the rejection of the prophet's warning, the speaking of a new ethical or secular "sign" of the future supplanting the prophet's sign, and the eventual acknowledgment of prophecy's fulfillment, but only with the hero's discovery of his own prophetic voice. The tragic transformations of this pattern reveal the political attitudes implicit in the epic version: on the one hand, a belief in the virtue of human speech as a sign of freedom and, on the other hand, the impulse to seize the power of the sign as a means to political control.

But why focus on the Theban plays of Sophocles, among the many Attic tragedies that portray the defiance of prophecy? Of the Greek tragedians, Euripides most explicitly criticizes the prophet's authority. In *Ion* he investigates both the reliability and the morality of Apollo's own prophecies in his shrine at Delphi. Yet Euripides is less interested than Sophocles in the heroic attitude toward the gods and their prophets, which is the concern of this book. Precisely because Euripides dismisses heroic defiance, I conclude with a consideration of Euripides' transformation of the figure of the prophet Tiresias in the *Phoenissae* and *Bacchae*, as well as his critique of the gods' signs and human stories in *Ion*. Thus I use Euripides to clarify the role of Sophocles' heroes as speakers and "readers."

Also deeply informed by prophecy, Aeschylus's plays might serve as my texts, especially *Seven Against Thebes* and the *Oresteia*, which depict the hero as an interpreter of prophecy. In *Seven Against Thebes*, the Messenger describes to Eteocles

---

6. See James Redfield, *Nature and Culture in the "Iliad": The Tragedy of Hector* (Chicago: University of Chicago Press, 1975), chap. 1, for a discussion of the *Iliad* as the "tragedy of Hector."

his enemies' seven shields, presented as omens of victory in the coming battle, but in response to each description Eteocles reinterprets the image to "predict" his own victory.[7] In the *Oresteia*, that magnificent web of prophetic dreams and omens, Orestes' task is to interpret in action Apollo's mandate and prophecy delivered at Delphi, and I discuss that "heroic" undertaking in Chapter 1.[8]

Yet Sophocles' Theban plays—*Antigone*, *Oedipus the King*, and *Oedipus at Colonus*—tell us more than any other Attic tragedies about the relationship between tragic heroism and the city's prophets. The story of the house of Laius is shaped by responses to prophecy. Laius fathers Oedipus, despite the Oracle's warning, yet abandons him in fear of it. The adopted Oedipus flees Corinth to avoid the disasters the Oracle predicted, yet comes to know himself only by taking on the Oracle's mandate to find Laius's murderer. At the end of his life, Oedipus finds his resting place at Colonus, just as Apollo predicted. After his and his sons' deaths, Oedipus's daughter Antigone defies Creon, Thebes' new leader, who scorns the prophet Tiresias once again. In telling this story in the first two plays (in the order of their composition), Sophocles sets the defiance of prophecy in the context of the problems of the city-state, particularly the threat of tyranny. But as Oedipus discovers his own prophetic voice in *Oedipus at Colonus*, Sophocles moves the scene of the hero's confrontation with prophecy to the city's boundaries and redefines the opposition between speech and silence, submission and authority, which characterizes the defiance of prophecy in the earlier plays.

This book defines the features of the tragic convention of prophecy, a familiar mark of the genre in Attic and later tragedy. The scene of the interpretation and fulfillment of prophecy recurs in plays written at a time when prophecy played an

7. See Froma Zeitlin, *Under the Sign of the Shield: Semiotics and Aeschylus' "Seven Against Thebes"* (Rome: Ateneo e Bizzari, 1982).

8. See Robert Fagles (with W. B. Stanford), "The Serpent and the Eagle," in *Aeschylus: The "Oresteia"* (New York: Viking, 1975), for this reading.

important political role. My concern is less with the specific historical context of an individual play of Sophocles—that is, with finding specific references or allegories—than with determining the historical value of prophecy itself, especially as it functioned in politics. This book examines the relationship between language and power in the discourse of prophecy and its use in Athenian politics and plays. It also investigates the problems raised by the valorization of the human voice and free speech in Western culture. If, as I suggest, the tradition of the tragic defiance of prophecy endows prophecy with characteristics more typical of writing than of speech, it makes that writing the enemy of the hero who must speak his own freedom. Prophecy, however, inscribed in the structure of plays, necessarily entraps the hero, unless or until he agrees to cooperate with it. Just as tragedy always presents a moral conflict between the strivings of the individual hero and the values of his community, it also conveys an ambivalence in regard to the value of free speech in city and state.

Since I started to write about prophecy in tragedy and epic, many people have helped and encouraged me. I am grateful to Robert Fagles, who inspired and challenged me, and to Froma Zeitlin, who has given advice, constant interest, and friendship.

Many others deserve thanks for their help: Gilbert Rose, my first teacher of Greek; Ann L. T. Bergren, who provided insight on Homer; and Georgia Nugent, who took time to talk about Sophocles. Istvan Csicsery-Ronay, Jr., Beverly Haviland, Rachel Hadas, Kevin Van Anglen, Ellen Pollak, Susan Snyder, and Peter Bing read parts or all of the manuscript and provided encouragement and wise advice. Kevin Kaplan toiled to check the references. I also owe much to Bernhard Kendler, to Allison Dodge for her skillful copyediting, and to several anonymous readers, but especially Robert Lamberton, a rigorous and kind reader for Cornell University Press. My mother-in-law, Ruth L. Toner, knows that I could not have written the book without her, and my lawyer, John Toner, counseled me in many crises.

I also thank the Mrs. Giles Whiting Foundation and the University of Pennsylvania, which provided the generous support that allowed me to write, research, and rewrite this book. Earlier versions of parts of Chapters 1 and 2 were published in *Helios* 9 (1982); passages of Chapters 2 and 3 appeared in *Classical and Modern Literature* 7 (1987); parts of Chapters 1 and 4 were published in *Classical and Modern Literature* 2 (1982) and in *Comparative Drama Annual*, vol. 5, *The Many Forms of Drama*, edited by Karelisa Hartigan (Lanham, Md.: University Press of America, 1985). I am grateful for permission to include this material here.

REBECCA W. BUSHNELL

Philadelphia, Pennsylvania

A Note on Texts, Translations, and Transliteration

I have quoted from the following texts, unless I have indicated otherwise:

Aeschyli: Septem Quae Supersunt Tragoedias. Ed. Denys Page. Oxford: Oxford University Press, 1972.

Aristotelis Politica. Ed. W. D. Ross. Oxford: Oxford University Press, 1957.

Euripidis Fabulae. Vols. 1 and 2 ed. J. Diggle; vol. 3 ed. Gilbert Murray. Oxford: Oxford University Press, 1981, 1984, 1913.

Herodoti Historiae. Ed. C. Hude. Oxford: Oxford University Press, 1927.

Homeri Opera. Ed. David B. Monro and Thomas W. Allen. 5 vols. Oxford: Oxford University Press, 1902–1920; rpt. 1966.

Platonis Opera. Ed. John Burnet. 5 vols. Oxford: Oxford University Press, 1900.

Sophoclis Fabulae. Ed. A. C. Pearson. Oxford: Oxford University Press, 1924; rpt. 1975. [I have also consulted *Sophoclis Tragoediae*, ed. R. D. Dawe, 2 vols. (Leipzig: Teubner, 1984). Any significant variants from Pearson are indicated in the notes.]

Thucydidis Historiae. Ed. H. S. Jones. Oxford: Oxford University Press, 1898.

Unless I have indicated otherwise, the translations are my own.

Short passages cited from the Greek texts are transliterated according to the *ALA Cataloguing Rules for Author and Title Entries* (Chicago: American Library Association, 1949). Iota subscripts are indicated in parentheses or brackets. Names of characters, however, appear in the forms by which they have become familiar to modern readers: Achilles, Hector, Creon, Polynices, and so on.

Prophesying
Tragedy

CHAPTER I

The Voice of Prophecy

In our own time, we have learned to be silent in the theater. We frown on those who talk or rustle their programs. We sit in the darkness, breaking our silence only with appropriate laughter or to acknowledge the end with our applause. That silence in the dark serves several purposes. It focuses our attention on the spectacle rather than on those around us, and it is our tribute of respect for the actors on the stage. Silence, in a more negative sense, signifies our passivity before the theatrical spectacle; as soon as the actors speak, in politeness we must hold our tongues. Yet silence is also a token of our power as an audience, for it may be our means of expressing disapproval when we know that we are expected to respond.

What is true of the theater is also true of the political arena. Both are places of public speech, in which our silence is a sign of our momentary difference from the politician or performer. When we cheer in approbation or hiss in anger, we remind the orator that we can violate that privilege of speech which we have implicitly bestowed; we can, after all, drown out the speaker if we disagree, although politeness will perhaps constrain many more now than it did in the past. At a political rally, as in the theater, silence may also be our way of withholding assent in response to the speaker's exhortations.

This tension between speech and silence which is felt in the theater, at the political rally, and at other places of public speaking is but one manifestation of the relationship of speech, politics, and power in Western society. Aristotle begins his *Politics* with the observation that man is by nature a political animal, because man alone of the animals can speak: "The mere voice [*phōnē*] signifies pain and pleasure," but all animals possess this voice; humans, however, master speech (*logos*) "to disclose what is useful and what is harmful, and the just and the unjust."[1] Aristotle here associates the ability to speak with the power to make moral judgments, insofar as both are basic to the foundation and operation of a polity. When humans make the distinction between good and bad, just and unjust, they do so in a community of household or state. The association of humans thus necessitates not just the existence but also the *pronouncement* of right and wrong. The difficulty of political association lies, indeed, in deciding who shall have the privilege to speak of what is right or wrong, in household or polity.

All Western theater is thus fundamentally political in that it represents human beings conversing, debating, and contending for the right to speak in the face of a silent—or perhaps not so silent—audience. Several recent studies of theater have connected theater and politics in terms of spectacle and performance. These studies follow the example of Clifford Geertz's work on the "theater states" of nineteenth-century Bali, where ceremony and ritual constituted a kind of "poetics of power."[2] The most basic link between Western theater and politics, however, is found in the representation and use of speech, because in Western culture speech is an integral part of both theatrical

---

1. Aristotle, *Politics* I.i.10–11 (1253a).
2. Clifford Geertz, *Negara: The Theatre State in Nineteenth-Century Bali* (Princeton: Princeton University Press, 1980), p. 123.

and political performance. More is at stake in theater and politics than just what language means; at the center of dramatic—particularly tragic—and political conflict is a contest for the *right to speak* both for oneself and for the city or state.[3] As Michel Foucault has said, "psychoanalysis has already shown us that speech is not merely the medium which manifests—or dissembles—desire; it is also the object of desire. Similarly, historians have constantly impressed upon us that speech is no mere verbalisation of conflicts and systems of domination, but that it is the very object of man's conflict."[4]

In theater and politics, public speech takes many forms, which differ rhetorically from what we might call everyday speech. The theatrical and political worlds of classical Athens shared an interest in the special language of prophecy, respecting it as a language of exceptional power. The use of prophecy in the plays and politics of Athens exemplifies the struggle for influence through control of public discourse, for the person who masters or controls the "divine" sign of prophecy may control the significance of events, in theater or marketplace.

Prophecy is a highly privileged form of speech, itself set off from ordinary political discourse in most societies. Most important, it is thought to bear a special kind of authority, the authority of divinity or inspiration. Humans fashion prophecy as the way divinity speaks to us about our own lives. Yet the language of prophecy is difficult and specialized, and we may misread it or fail to recognize it as meaningful. The features we attribute to this divine language are the ones that trouble us most in our own language. Ambiguity, for example, rep-

---

3. See also Jonathan Goldberg, "Shakespearean Inscriptions: The Voicing of Power," in *Shakespeare and the Question of Theory*, ed. Patricia Parker and Geoffrey Hartman (New York: Methuen, 1985), pp. 116–137: "Authority in the Shakespearean text is a matter not of having a voice but of voicing. This is the field of history, a stage of power" (p. 119).

4. Michel Foucault, "The Discourse on Language," in *The Archaeology of Language*, trans. A. M. Sheridan Smith (New York: Harper & Row, 1972), p. 216.

resents the way in which language is ultimately out of our control; the assumed irreversibility of the prophetic word reminds us how words may exercise control in other contexts. As speech, prophecy is paradoxically riddled with silences. Omens, as iconic signs, are of course silent, and oracles, while they seem to speak to us in our own language, are full of unspoken meanings. Silence within such speech is less a token of passivity or weakness than a source of power in the face of human efforts to speak and respond.

Among the kinds of literature generated in the political and prophetic worlds of classical Athens, tragedy is the genre in which the power of the human voice is most apparently opposed to the powers of "fatal" prophecy and silence. Tragic and epic prophecy and fate reflect not some mysterious compulsion but ultimately the plot's shape, or the fixed shape of legend or history.[5] When we are troubled by the contradiction between the Homeric Zeus's omnipotence and his subservience to fate, Cedric Whitman would remind us that these categories are, after all, "modes of speaking"; "The fate which [Zeus] must acknowledge is the poet's scenario viewed as ineluctable fact, and herein lies the meaning of the frequent phrases 'according to fate' and 'contrary to fate.' "[6] Thus fate seems external and compelling only when a character is shown as resenting the circumstances the reader or audience recognizes as "fact" or "history." According to Northrop Frye, "fate, in a tragedy, normally becomes external to the hero only *after* the tragic process has been set going. The Greek *ananke* or *moira* is in its normal, or pretragic, form the internal balancing condition of life. It appears as external or antithetical necessity only after it has been violated as a condition of life, just as

5. See James Redfield, *Nature and Culture in the "Iliad": The Tragedy of Hector* (Chicago: University of Chicago Press, 1975), pp. 133–35, on fate as "plot," history, and nature. See also Cedric H. Whitman, *Homer and the Heroic Tradition* (Cambridge: Harvard University Press, 1958; rpt. New York: Norton, 1965), chap. 10.

6. Whitman, *Homer and the Heroic Tradition*, p. 228.

justice is the internal condition of the honest man, but the external antagonist of the criminal."[7]

In tragedy, the oracle, prophecy, or omen functions as the sign of the tragic plot in which the hero plays the role assigned to him in myth, legend, or history. The oracular sign, like the "fate" it represents, may entail a kind of necessity, but this is the necessity of conflict rather than acquiescence. In *The Origin of German Tragic Drama*, Walter Benjamin defines oracular necessity in these terms:

> The oracle in tragedy is more than just a magical incantation of fate; it is a projection of the certainty that there is no tragic life which does not take place in its framework. The necessity which appears to be built into the framework is neither a causal nor a magical necessity. It is the unarticulated necessity of defiance, in which the self brings forth its utterances.[8]

Some tragedians may have prophets speak, and their prophecies fulfilled, to give "the beginning [of their plays] some symmetrical relationship with the end";[9] but above all, prophets speak in tragedies so that heroes may defy them and thus define themselves in speaking the prophet's contradiction. It is the rule of fate's game that, insofar as omen or oracle represents the story or plot, it must come true, according to the social values associated with the representation of fate; it is also true, however, that Greek society valorized that act of heroic self-definition.

This tragic conflict cannot be separated or isolated from the value and role given to prophecy in the culture that produced Attic tragedy. The hero's defiance of augury, representing a

7. Northrop Frye, *Anatomy of Criticism: Four Essays* (1957; rpt. Princeton: Princeton University Press, 1971), p. 210.

8. Walter Benjamin, *The Origin of German Tragic Drama*, trans. John Osborne (London: NLB, 1977), p. 115. See also "Fate and Character," in *Reflections*, ed. Peter Demetz, trans. E. Jepcott (New York: Harcourt Brace Jovanovich, 1978).

9. Frye, p. 139.

clash between hero and god for the right to bespeak the future, intersects with the political conflicts of fifth-century Athens, especially because politics directly involved the use or abuse of prophecy. The hero who defies prophecy, rejecting, misreading, or obliterating the divine sign, sees himself as reacting against a language of authority, which "prescribes" his life. In this way, the tragic hero's speaking out against the gods' privileged signs identifies his freedom with *his* speech, for in the Western tradition, as Derrida says, "speech always presents itself as the best expression of liberty."[10]

When the hero speaks out against his enslavement to the divine sign, his opposition also reflects a more general cultural and political crisis of authority in those Attic tragedies that dramatize the tensions of a society preoccupied with problems of human responsibility, language, religious authority, and tyranny. More specifically, the hero's experience with prophecy reflects not only his response to the language of the gods but also a reaction to prophecy's involvement in the political life of Athens. While in tragedy the fulfillment of oracle or omen was taken as the sign of a divinely willed or foreseen plot, in political intrigue an oracle or omen might be invented or appropriated to sanction a political maneuver or plot. It is thus not surprising that in tragedy the hero's trial of the prophet commonly occurs in the context of a political rebellion or crisis in city or state. The threat to the gods' tyranny is associated with political instability or a challenge to a current government. When heroes defy the tyranny of the gods, they do so in the belief that they can control their own lives, but also, in Attic tragedy, they do so to gain control of state or city. They themselves may thus verge on the tyrannical in their desire to appropriate the power of signs. On the one hand, tragedy

10. Jacques Derrida, *Of Grammatology*, trans. Gayatri Chakravorty Spivak (1967; rpt. Baltimore: Johns Hopkins University Press, 1976), p. 168. Derrida's critique of the opposition between speech and writing in Western metaphysics and linguistics underlies my discussion of divine writing and human speech.

celebrates the heroic will to defy authority as it is represented by prophecy; on the other hand, such an act of defiance implies the hero's desire to seize power for himself, in city or state. Tragedy denies the hero a power like that of the gods, granting him freedom and autonomy only on the city's boundaries or on the border between life and death itself.

Homeric epic clearly differentiates the language the gods use in prophecy and the "ordinary" speech used by humans, setting a pattern that persists in Attic tragedy and that is basic to the formulation of the ethical and political significance of the conflict between hero and prophet. In Homeric epic, prophecy is conveyed mostly through natural omens, prodigies, and disturbances of the heavens, which threaten and console wondering mortals. In the *Iliad*, the nature and function of omens are most clearly seen in the many bird signs, which constitute a language whose apparent simplicity masks its complex conventions and unique temporality.

What makes a bird a sign in Homeric epic? As Eurymachos reminds Halitherses in the *Odyssey* (2.181–82), not all birds are ominous (*enaisimoi*): a bird, like other natural phenomena, becomes a sign by differentiation according to convention and context. It may be significant because it is a predator[11] or because it is conventionally recognized as a messenger of a particular deity.[12] It may also be differentiated by its abnormal or "prodigious" actions: such are the eagles that tear at each

11. The bird of prey functions best as a sign for two reasons: first, because it flies alone, and so its action is single; and second, because its mode of action, one of violent assault, invites comparison with human actions in a violent world. A. Bouché-Leclercq, in *Histoire de la divination dans l'antiquité* (Paris: Leroux, 1879–82), relates divination by the flight of predators to the practice of haruspicy (see vol. 1, pp. 129–30).

12. The *aietos*, or "eagle," is the favorite bird of Zeus throughout Greek literature and myth. The *kirkos*, or "hawk," is identified as a messenger of Apollo (*Odyssey* 15.526). In *Iliad* 10.272–77, Athena is said to send an *erōdios*, "heron," to Odysseus and Diomedes. The heron was recognized as a symbol of Athena, according to D'arcy Thompson, *A Glossary of Greek Birds* (Oxford: Oxford University Press, 1936), p. 103.

other's head in *Odyssey* 2.146–55, and the sparrows eaten by the snake in *Iliad* 2.308–20.[13] Context, too, plays a role in the "significance" of a bird: a bird whose actions are normal may signify if the context in which it appears represents a deviation from the normal order of events. Hildebrand Stockinger suggests that in almost all cases in Homer, omens appear when a sacrifice is being performed or a prayer or wish is expressed, that is, when humans are "in communion" with the gods.[14] Exceptions to Stockinger's rule include omens that appear at points of transition in the action, such as setting out on a journey or crossing a critical line in battle, which are also "marked" events in the flow of action.[15]

The ornithomantic sign is thus fundamentally conventional, rather than natural; that is, a bird becomes significant in a structure of differences, through its species or behavior, or its appearance in a situation that differs from the ordinary course of events.[16] Yet once the sign is recognized as such, the sign's

---

13. Raymond Bloch, in *Les Prodiges dans l'antiquité classique* (Paris: Presses Universitaires de France, 1963), defines this kind of prodigy as "the invasion of the sacred into the profane, testifying to some sort of modification of the relations between men and gods" (p. 2).

14. Hildebrand Stockinger, *Die Vorzeichen im Homerischen Epos: Ihre Typik und Ihre Bedeutung* (St. Ottilien, Oberbayern: EOS, 1959). Stockinger uses as evidence for this generalization such scenes as that in *Iliad* 2.308–20, when the omen of the snake and sparrows appears in the midst of the sacrifice at Aulis; that in *Odyssey* 20.98–104, when Odysseus prays for signs both inside and outside the house; and that in *Odyssey* 15.160–65, when upon Telemachus's wishing that he could show Odysseus the treasure he received from Menelaus, an eagle bearing a goose descends on his right.

15. Examples of such omens include the bird that appears to the Trojans as they are about to cross the Achaians' ditch (*Iliad* 12.195–229) and the heron that appears to Diomedes and Odysseus as they are setting out on their night raid (*Iliad* 10.272–77).

16. In this respect, the Homeric classification of bird signs resembles that of the Iban of South Borneo as described by Claude Levi-Strauss in *The Savage Mind* (1962; English trans., Chicago: University of Chicago Press, 1966): "Arbitrary as it seems when only its individual terms are considered, the system becomes coherent when it is seen as a whole set.... The terms never have any intrinsic significance. Their meaning is one of 'position'—a function of the history and cultural context on the one hand and of the structural system in which they are called upon to appear on the other" (pp. 54–55).

interpreter characteristically makes an appeal to nature, which masks the sign's conventionality. In Homeric epic, where the only obvious conventional key to reading a bird sign is the direction of the bird's flight with respect to the observer,[17] the *mantis* or prophet bases his interpretation less on "decoding" than on drawing analogies between the bird's "natural" behavior—its actions and appearance—and the relevant aspects of the human affairs to which the sign is related.

In his study of analogical thought in the *Odyssey*, Norman Austin compares the interpretation of omens to Homeric similes, in that omens are "similes that are the property of the characters in the poems rather than of the poet."[18] The relationship between the omen and its significance may be said to correspond to the relationship between the "vehicle" and the "tenor" of the Homeric simile.[19] In a typical simile, the poet says of Poseidon that he rose to fly "as (*hōs*) does a swift winged hawk, which lifting from the steep high rock, pursues another bird over the wide plain; so (*hōs*) the earthshaker Poseidon broke away from them" (*Iliad* 13.62–65). Here the bird's flight is the "vehicle," Poseidon's motion the "tenor." One might compare Helen's interpretation of an *oiōnos* ("bird sign") in *Odyssey* 15.174–78:

As [*hōs*] this [eagle] seized the goose, reared in the house,
Coming from the mountain, where he was born, and his
offspring are,

17. Homeric ornithomancy must in the end be distinguished from later practice, for which we have historical evidence. Bouché-Leclercq, pp. 135–41, reviews the evidence in the work of Alexandrian scholars, which suggests that in its later development ornithomancy was based on a strict code of binary oppositions. The reading of the sign was based on the direction of the bird's flight, its species, cry, seat or perch, and mode of action. W. R. Halliday, in *Greek Divination* (London: Macmillan, 1913), pp. 270–71, comments on Bouché-Leclercq's evidence for ornithomantic practice among the Greeks.

18. Norman Austin, *Archery at the Dark of the Moon: Poetic Problems in Homer's "Odyssey"* (Berkeley: University of California Press, 1975), p. 118.

19. The terminology of "vehicle" and "tenor" is, of course, that of I. A. Richards, in *The Philosophy of Rhetoric* (New York: Oxford University Press, 1936).

So [*hōs*] Odysseus, having suffered many evils and much
   wandered,
Will return and take revenge.

Helen uses here the *hōs/hōs* idiom of the Homeric simile; the
bird's actions are, in effect, the "vehicle" and her "interpretation" (Odysseus's future actions) the "tenor." Like the simile,
the omen and its interpretation thus function as the "assimi-
lation of one unified structure into another" in an effort to
integrate the human, divine, and natural worlds.[20] In
the process of thought that governs both simile and omen,
it appears that god, human, and bird act according to the same
laws: there seems to be a "natural" and not merely conventional connection between vehicle and tenor, omen and
interpretation.
   This interpretive method tempts the reader to see a kind of
magical or fatal power of causation in the Homeric omen and
to assume that in the archaic period everyone believed that
such omens *cause* human events. Robert Flacelière, for example, writes that credulity in omens can be explained as "a
survival of a primitive mentality" according to which "extraordinary behavior on the part of animals (who for a long time
had been worshipped as gods) could determine what was to
come to pass among men.... Thus the marvelous omen was
not merely a sign of what was going to happen, essentially it
was its cause; the omen and its fulfillment were fatally connected by a bond that could not be dissolved by prayer or any
other religious rite."[21] In Homeric epic, however, there are
those—both impious and heroic men—who insist that not all
birds are ominous; they remind us that the link between bird
and human is made by the prophet and is not found in "nature." Just as Redfield and Whitman have demystified the no-
tion of Homeric fate, redefining it as plot or history, so these

signs of fate are subject to the skepticism of the epic's characters and audience alike.

The Homeric language of omens is distinguished not only by its conventionality, which may be masked as "nature," but also by its problematic temporality. The Homeric omen is characteristically ephemeral, not inscribed in stone;[22] in this sense it resembles the spoken word. Because the omen usually appears in response to a human prayer or boast, it seems to participate in a "dialogue" in a speaking "present."[23] Thus in *Iliad* 24, when Priam prays to Zeus to send a sign confirming that he should go to ransom Hector, Zeus sends an eagle as an affirmation (301–21). When a sign is not definitely requested in prayer but appears in response to a boast, sacrifice, or other direct or implied statement about the future, it generally refers to present circumstances or to the immediate future. Such a sign most frequently is an affirmation, but sometimes is a denial; thus the sign itself is taken as a prediction of the future.

This appears to be a simple system, but it allows many opportunities for misreading. For example, one can mistake a denial for an affirmation, or vice versa, although in most cases a sign's import is clarified by its appearance on the right or left side of the observer. More commonly, there is confusion about the temporal significance of omens, as when Zeus makes his thunder sign in *Iliad* 8. 167–76. Zeus thunders three times when Diomedes hesitates thrice about whether to fight Hector, who has boasted that Diomedes will never overcome him, and take his city. The poet says that by this sign Zeus informs the Trojans that the tide of battle is turning. The context makes it clear that Zeus is not responding to Hector's boast that

22. The one exception is the omen of the sparrows and snake that are turned to stone, reported in *Iliad* 2.

23. See Emile Benveniste, *Problèmes de linguistique générale* (Paris: Gallimard, 1966), on the idea that the present tense is defined in the moment of speaking: "This present tense has no other temporal reference than a linguistic given: the coincidence of the event described with the discourse that describes it" (p. 262, translation mine).

Diomedes will never conquer Troy but is referring only to the immediate future of the battle. Yet Hector misreads the thunder as Zeus's promise of support throughout the war.

In the case of the bird sign of the battling eagle and the snake in *Iliad* 12.201–27, which appears when the Trojans are about to breach the Achaians' wall, a similar confusion of temporality occurs. There, no word has been spoken when the sign appears; instead, the Trojans are about to make a move on which the future of the war depends. No reference is made to Zeus's agency in sending the sign, but its divine origin is suggested by its prodigious nature and its relevance to the immediate future is derived from the analogous features of the narrative. Polydamas, Hector's most vocal adviser, interprets the sign in a narrow temporal context, extrapolating from the eagle's and snake's behavior that the Trojans will not return home safely if they breach the wall, but Hector takes its significance in a broader context, as a general counsel of retreat—one he must reject.

Such scenes expose the limitations of the divine language of omens in relation to "human" discourse. While the omen may have a narrowly defined present tense and an implied future tense, it lacks a *gnomic* present. Designed only to foretell specific events, it does not speak of eternal truths. Certainly in Homeric epic the immortal gods are not in the habit of making timeless statements, however far into time they might see. In these poems, it is humans who are generally given the gnomic voice. The heroic misreading or defiance of the sign betrays a dissatisfaction with the provisional nature of divine discourse—and perhaps with the imperfect and inconsistent gods themselves. In epic, it is humans, not the gods, who speak of and long for absolute, timeless value and meaning.

In Greek tragedy, the value and terms of prophecy differ from those of epic. The difference is found in the representation of the gods and in the new emphasis on oracles over omens, but the epic characteristics of the conventions and temporality of divine signs persist. The Olympians appear less frequently in Attic tragedy, and speak differently from the Homeric gods.

Only in some of the plays of Aeschylus and Euripides do the Olympian gods speak before the audience. The gods appear in only two of Aeschylus's extant plays, *Prometheus Bound* and the *Eumenides*. In the *Eumenides* the representation of the gods is closest to that of Homer; the appearance of Apollo and Athena on stage is, indeed, an emblem of divine sponsorship and concern for humanity, as we find it in Homer. While the gods appear more frequently in Euripides' plays than in those of Aeschylus and Sophocles, their arrival and their relationships with those mortals whose lives they govern are almost always problematic. In Sophocles' plays, the figure of deity almost disappears from the stage altogether, with the exception of Athena's appearance in *Ajax* and the role of Heracles deified as an Olympian in *Trachiniae* and *Philoctetes*. In the Theban plays, divinity is present only in oracles and signs and in the voice of the prophet. The gods of Sophocles have become more impersonal than the Homeric gods; increasingly, they are identified with inexorable fate, rather than simply represented as having access to knowledge of the future. Of course, this representation of the gods reflects changes in religious beliefs, but it also suggests a peculiarly tragic idea of how the gods communicate with humans.

In its frequent use of oracles, tragedy reflects a change in the historical practice of divination, or communication with the gods; the consultant's interaction with the Delphic Oracle and other oracles was considered to be an advance over older, inductive forms of divination. Oracular consultation seemed to permit virtually direct communication between god and mortal. Jean-Pierre Vernant describes that change in attitude in the fifth century B.C.:

> The Greeks valorized oral divination; instead of techniques of interpretation of signs, procedures of the aleatory type such as the throwing of dice, which they considered minor forms, they preferred what R. Crahay calls the oracular dialogue, in which the god's word responds directly to the ques-

tions of the consultant. . . . Unlike the interpretation of omens
or procedures of technical divination, which required the
services of a specialized prophet, the oracular language of
the gods, once formulated, is, like any other language, accessible to everyone; to understand it, one does not need
special competence in matters of divination.[24]

While in Homeric epic, a conflict may arise between prophet
and hero because the sign is mute until it is given a voice by
one who claims to understand its language, historically, when
Apollo gave an oracle through the Pythia, he delivered a text
apparently accessible to all speakers of Greek.[25] In Greek tragedy, however, even in the simpler, more straightforward oracles
such as we find in the Theban plays, accessibility is an illusion,
functioning to mislead the consultant.

At first, it would seem that in tragedy, too, oracular language
differs little from ordinary language; the gods speak in a human
tongue, rather than through omens. But the divine oracle uses
a privileged language that can deceive those who treat it as if
it were ordinary speech. Although oracular communication
seems like dialogue, as Crahay and Vernant suggest, the oracle,
unlike the human speaker, will state the "facts" but not interpret the causes, mechanism, or results of those circumstances.
Once uttered, the oracular response more closely resembles
written text than speech, according to Plato's description of
writing in the *Phaedrus*.[26] Writing is like the products of paint-

24. Jean-Pierre Vernant, "Paroles et signes muets," in Vernant et al., *Divination et rationalité* (Paris: Seuil, 1974), pp. 18–19. Translation mine.

25. I am convinced by the argument of Joseph Fontenrose, *The Delphic
Oracle: Its Responses and Operations with a Catalogue of Responses* (Berkeley: University of California Press, 1978), pp. 126–228, that the Pythia spoke
clearly and directly to the enquirer, rather than in wild cries that had to be
interpreted by the priest.

26. See Charles Segal, "Greek Tragedy: Writing, Truth and the Representation of the Self," in *Interpreting Greek Tragedy: Myth, Poetry, Text* (Ithaca:
Cornell University Press, 1986), on the significance of writing in culture. Segal
says: "The further development of writing increases the duplicitous potential
of language. The gap between word and thing, logos and ergon, between
what one says and what one is, becomes ever more evident and more prob-
lematical" (p. 93).

ing, says Socrates, because paintings look as if they are living, but if you ask them something, "they keep a solemn silence" (*semnōs pany siga*[i]). "Such are written words: they appear as if having thought they have something to say, but if you talk to them, wanting to learn something of what they say, they always signify the one and same thing."[27] This relationship between the oracle and its consultant is implicitly a relationship of power and subjection, as the oracle's questioner, trapped by silence, is forced to answer for himself how, when, and why; he must break the oracle's silence with human speech. Walter Benjamin contrasts speech and writing in a way that suggests the opposition between the hero's "free speech" and the gods' "allegorical" and "written" oracular language:

> The spoken word, it might be said, is the ecstasy of the creature; it is exposure, rashness, powerlessness before God; the written word is the composure of the creature, dignity, superiority, omnipotence over the objects of the world.... Spoken language is thus the domain of the free, spontaneous utterance of the creature, whereas the written language of allegory enslaves objects in the eccentric embrace of meaning.[28]

Thus, although in the tragedies considered here the oracle's and prophet's language itself does not seem particularly spectacular or riddling, oracular writing is distinguished from human speech specifically by its ominous silences: what the hero fears in the god's words and what he often cannot hear. These are the silences of writing whereby, in Charles Segal's words, "language now is no longer the fullness of ready, serviceable stories that flow from the generous gifts of goddess memory; it becomes an ambiguous series of signs, traces, and absences."[29] On closer examination, the features of tragic prophetic language closely resemble those of the silent Homeric

27. *Phaedrus* 275d. See Richard Goodkin, "Tracing the Trace: Oedipus and Derrida," *Helios* 9 (1982): 15–27.
28. Benjamin, p. 202.
29. Segal, p. 93.

language of omens: a subtle play with convention and a manipulation of temporality.

Like the language of ornithomancy, oracular language manipulates the polysemy inherent in conventional signification. In Homeric epic, a bird may be just that: a creature of nature, such as those that haunt Calypso's island (*Odyssey* 5.65–67); but some birds convey a message of the gods, which has little relation to their "natural" significance. It is in this sense that Homeric bird signs are polysemic, not only because any bird sign may have many interpretations, but also because a bird can be both a thing in nature and a divine sign. Oracular language, too, uses homonymy, in cases when "the recipient understands a name or word in its familiar or accepted sense, but it has an unexpected or obscure meaning."[30] Joseph Fontenrose relates an interesting example of such a twist: "Daphidas [a Sophist], wanting to make the Delphic Apollo look ridiculous, asked the god whether he would find his horse, although he had neither lost a horse nor owned one. The god replied that he would find his *hippos*, but, as one version adds, would be thrown from it and die.... So Daphidas thought he had tricked the Delphic god; but soon afterwards King Attalos of Pergamon had him thrown from a cliff called Hippos."[31] Here the oracle seems to force a double meaning where one would never expect it: the word for horse, *hippos*, is given a second, discrete referent as a place name. This oracular polysemy is analogous to the ambiguity of signs in Homeric epic, where the appearance of a bird is given a discrete referent in its prophetic interpretation. All such oracles that exploit polysemy mask a secondary meaning with an apparently accessible surface meaning, luring the recipient into a "false sense of security," in that he thinks he understands and is communicating with the god.[32]

---

30. Fontenrose, pp. 62–63.
31. Fontenrose, pp. 60–61.
32. Fontenrose, p. 63.

The power of oracular speech, like that of bird signs, is also involved in its representation of time. The amateur interpreter of the bird sign is confused by the relationship of the mute sign to its immediate context and implied future context. While oracular temporality is far more difficult to describe than that of the bird sign, the most familiar confusion of oracular temporality occurs when one future event is said to coincide with another, in a kind of riddling hypotaxis. In a famous legendary example, Croesus, when he asked how long he should reign, was told by the Pythia that he would be king until a mule became king of the Medes. To Croesus this seemed tantamount to a promise that his reign would last forever, but of course the oracle meant that he would reign only until Cyrus the "mule"—half Persian and half Mede—ascended the throne.[33] In this case, in answer to a question about time, the oracle made a limited period of time sound like eternity.

Other oracles reflect the temporality of riddles in which the natural laws of time are overthrown. The Sphinx's riddle, for example, compresses the three ages of man into a monster of simultaneity, a two-footed, three-footed, and four-footed beast. So, too, in Sophocles' *Trachiniae* the oracle of Zeus at Dodona is said to have told Heracles he should not be killed by any but one who is already dead. When Heracles dies by infection from Nessos's poisoned blood, what seems impossible in terms of time and nature becomes possible. Oracular language thus characteristically twists the natural sequence of human events.

In contrast to the omens of epic, oracles in Greek tragedy may reflect the image of an ideal, eternal divinity in their permanence, their tangible and ineradicable mark as "text,"[34] and may also suggest that the gods are concerned enough about

33. Herodotus 1.55.2.
34. See Fontenrose, pp. 218–19: "The priest-prophet who attended the Pythia presided over the mantic session at Delphi, answering all questions except the question put to the Pythia as the gods' mouthpiece. He probably put the Pythia's response in writing and delivered a copy to the messengers of absent enquirers."

human affairs to send advice and information in a language that can be understood. Yet the oracle in tragedy, like the bird sign, remains at heart elusive in its ambiguity and twisted time and in its silence. Plato saw a contradiction in attributing ambiguous language to the gods: How could ideal and perfect beings speak such an imperfect language? In reality, he claimed, "a god is simple, true in word and deed, and neither changes himself nor deceives others with apparitions, or words, or the sending of signs, whether in dreams or not."[35] The tragic hero is made to criticize the tragic gods' language in similar terms, questioning whether the privileged and "lying" discourse of the gods has any significance for him.

For the fifth-century audiences of Attic tragedy, the representation of the gods' prophetic language in tragedy was set against the role of the Delphic Oracle and other important oracle sites in Athenian politics and culture, as well as the practices of more ad hoc prophets, the *chrēsmologoi*, or "oracle peddlers." As we read the plays the Athenians saw, it would seem to us that the fulfillment of oracular predictions in plays and politics provided a structure and meaning for otherwise apparently random human events.[36] The pious could be content that things happen as they do because the gods predicted them:[37]the realization of prophecy represented an ordered and stable world. The historical situation, however, was rather more complicated, for not only were many Greeks skeptical about prophecy, but they also saw how people might manipulate oracles to create the impression that a certain action was part of the divine order.

Tragic prophecy does imply a divine order, or as Northrop

---

35. *Republic* 2.382e.

36. This is the conclusion reached by Deborah H. Roberts in *Apollo and His Oracle in the "Oresteia"* (Goettingen: Vandenhoeck & Ruprecht, 1984). Without focusing on the political uses of oracles, Roberts argues convincingly that oracles fulfill a need for order and closure.

37. See Bernard Knox, *Oedipus at Thebes* (New Haven: Yale University Press, 1957; rpt. New York: Norton, 1971), pp. 47–48.

Frye puts it, "a conception of ineluctable fate or hidden om-
nipotent will," even if "the only ineluctable will involved is
that of the author."[38] In some plays, the fulfillment of prophecy
informs the entire plot. In Aeschylus's *Persians*, for example,
the action consists in the telling of prophetic dreams and nec-
romantic oracles and the report of their fulfillment. The
Queen's narration of her vision is swiftly followed by the Messenger's story of the Persians' defeat, and Darius's prediction
of the army's destruction brings on the entrance of Xerxes,
bereft of followers. In other plays, a character's recognition of
an oracle's fulfillment enables him or her to bring the action
to a conclusion. In Sophocles' *Trachiniae*, Heracles rages in
confusion until he realizes that the prophecy has come true,
that indeed he will die at the hands of one already dead. Once
Heracles understands this, he accepts that his end has come
and calmly orders Hyllus to prepare his pyre. Thus, in this case,
by recognizing the oracle's fulfillment, the character himself
imposes order and brings the play to its conclusion. Attic com-
edy mocks the "authorial" or authoritative function of dramatic oracles by associating them with the *chrēsmologoi* rather
than with the Delphic Oracle. In Aristophanes' *Knights*, when
the villain Paphlagon (Kleon) and the Sausage Seller hero reach
a stalemate in their battle for Demos's favor, Paphlagon suddenly capitulates when he discovers that the Sausage Seller
matches the description of his nemesis found in the oracle
books. Here the oracle's parodistic style and exaggerated lack
of motivation call attention to its use as a formal dramatic
device: Aristophanes parodies the use of oracles as a kind of
linguistic deus ex machina, playfully exposing the playwright's
authority as Apollo's surrogate.

   This dramatic technique, whereby the playwright exercises
his "authority" in the creation and fulfillment of prophecy, has
been associated with an orthodox Athenian piety, which saw
the fulfillment of oracles as a sign of divine omnipresence in

38. Frye, p. 139.

human lives. No historian would deny that the Delphic Oracle, which appears so frequently in tragedy, had great importance as a religious authority in Hellenic culture, especially for the establishment of cult. Plato, for one, stresses the Delphic Oracle's role in instituting the religious order of his Republic. He insists that such matters as the locations of temples, funerals, sacrifices, and worship be decided by Apollo at Delphi: "For we do not understand these things, and in founding our city, if we are sensible, we shall trust them to no other, nor use any other oracle than that of our fathers."[39] As this passage suggests, the Delphic Oracle played an important role in Greek colonization, particularly in furnishing the founders of cities with "ritual laws for religious cults and institutions to be established overseas."[40]

The Oracle's role in the political life of fifth-century Athens, however, raises more problems for historians. Until recently, scholars mostly investigated the question of the Oracle's political independence after the Persian Wars.[41] Now, Crahay, Fontenrose, and other scholars challenge the assumption that the Oracle really offered "the kind of oracles that Herodotus quotes, those spoken to Croesus or to the Spartans on Tegea or to the Greek states at the time of the Persian Wars."[42] These scholars believe that the Oracle's *historical* pronouncements were rather straightforward, uncomplicated recommendations on matters of ritual and cult. They insist that the Oracle's well-known *political* predictions were mostly later inventions, in imitation of folkloric riddles or prophecy; these predictions did not originate with the Delphic Oracle but were later attributed to it as it became more prestigious. What we find in Herodotus, according to Crahay and Fontenrose, are oracles borrowed or invented to *explain* historical circumstances,[43] to give shape

---

39. Plato, *Republic* 4.427.
40. Flacelière, p. 56.
41. Flacelière, p. 58.
42. Fontenrose, p. 6.

and meaning to human history after the event. It appears that the Oracle's stature as a "predictor" owed more to its reputation than to actual practice.

One must ask, of course, whether the Athenians themselves saw a distinction between the "genuine" and "legendary" pronouncements of the Oracle. Did they accept all its oracles, past and present, unconditionally, or did they admit that some were useful inventions? Few scholars deny that in the fifth century at least some people doubted the value of prophecy and that many were aware of the political exploitation of oracles concerning civic affairs.[44] Skepticism was certainly present, if not prevalent: Euripides attacked prophets in his plays, and the rationalists and Sophists criticized any belief in supernatural phenomena.[45] While the collections of oracles peddled by *chrēsmologoi* were more commonly ridiculed, even Apollo's oracle was open to attack.[46] Jocasta's and Oedipus's efforts to discredit prophecy in *Oedipus the King* can be related to the evidence of skepticism regarding oracles and signs in fifth-century Athens.[47] Whitman, for example, associates Jocasta's opinions on prophecy with "the 'intelligent piety' of the Periclean circle," where it was believed that "signs and wonders may not be devoid of meaning, but they must not command our minds."[48]

43. See Roland Crahay, *La Littérature oraculaire chez Hérodote* (Paris: Belles Lettres, 1956): "First the oracle can explain facts of obscure origin: a ritual, the epithet of a god, the location of a temple, the presence or nature of an object, the name of a city. It provides its explanations by one of its characteristic methods: story theme, riddle, wordplay. The reported event matters less—it is the conclusion that is important" (p. 59, translation mine).

44. Flacelière, pp. 60–72.

45. Knox, pp. 44–45.

46. On *chrēsmologoi*, see Flacelière, pp. 61–65; Fontenrose, pp. 144–65; and Martin P. Nilsson, *Cults, Myths, Oracles, and Politics in Ancient Greece* (Lund: Gleerup, 1951), pp. 130–42. For attacks on the Delphic Oracle, see Flacelière, pp. 70–71.

47. See Knox, pp. 44–45, and Cedric H. Whitman, *Sophocles: A Study of Heroic Humanism* (Cambridge: Harvard University Press, 1951), pp. 135–36.

48. Whitman, *Sophocles*, p. 136.

Perhaps more than any other Athenian writer we know, Thucydides was distrustful of prophecy and omens.[49] He describes an *ex eventu* interpretation of an oracle during the Athenian plague in 430 B.C., when the people remembered an old oracle that had predicted that "a Dorian war shall come and with it death" (*hexei dōriakos polemos kai loimos ham' auto[i]*). As he says, the people began to argue whether *loimos* ("death") or *limos* ("famine") had been the word in the old verse, but decided in favor of *loimos*, the current catastrophe. Thucydides dryly remarks that the people remembered according to what they suffered, but he imagines that if someday there should be a Dorian war, and famine should occur, the word will be remembered as *limos*.[50] Thucydides thus stresses that it is not only unscrupulous oracle-peddlers who shape oracles to their liking: so do all humans in their efforts to make sense of their lives. This climate of suspicion of oracular authority opens up the opportunity for anyone to seize the power attributed to prophecy, in both plays and politics; certainly the oracular authority is not so secure as it seems on the surface.

The function of the Delphic Oracle and of prophetic interpretation in Aeschylus's *Oresteia* offers an interesting example of the tension between the manipulation of oracles and their interpretation, on the one hand, and the use of oracles to create closure and a sense of divine order, on the other. Deborah Roberts has written of the oracles in the *Oresteia* that "the desire for fulfillment of oracles as a desire to see an order and structure in things over time is relevant not only to the stress placed on the oracle within the story of the *Oresteia* but to its use in ending the play, in bringing closure to the drama as well as the action represented in the drama."[51] As she suggests, that closure is not entirely fixed because of the fundamental am-

---

49. For a citation of historians who agree on this subject and for an opposing view, see Nanno Marinatos, *Thucydides and Religion* (Koenigstein: Anton Hain, 1981).

50. Thucydides ii.54.

51. Roberts, p. 122.

biguity of the figure of the sublime and destructive Apollo. It is also threatened by the instability of prophecy throughout the first half of the trilogy, especially as Clytemnestra uses it quite self-consciously as a means of fashioning her own authority.[52]

Clytemnestra's use of prophecy in *Agamemnon* suggests that in her "primitive" world, power lies in the ability to manipulate a sign's form and its interpretation. Clytemnestra masters signs as well as speech, a power exemplified in her control over the beacons that fire the news of Troy's fall from Ilium to Argos. The play makes it a mark of her rule of Argos that she both creates and interprets the beacons. "I arranged [ordained] this bearing of lights" (*Agamemnon* 312), she says; as she created them, they are her *symbolon* (which can mean "omen" as well as "secret code" or "symbol") and her *tekmar* ("sure sign," 315), sent from Troy to her.[53] The Chorus seems fascinated by her sign and asks to hear the story again. She responds with a vision of Troy's fall, which amounts to a reading or interpretation of her sign of the defeat, a reading that is a very biased version of the conquering heroes' inhumanity and impiety. The Chorus ratifies the reading and the sign as trustworthy (*pista sou tekmēria*) and authoritative, as well as manly and wise (351–54). Thus by accepting both sign and reading they are granting her real authority in Argos, as Agamemnon's substitute, and symbolic power, as one who foresees and sees through events.

An essential part of the *Oresteia*'s ideological "progress," of course, involves replacing Clytemnestra's voice and foresight with those of Apollo.[54] The oracle of Apollo at Delphi is the

52. I am grateful to Elizabeth Magnus for sharing her unpublished work on the political manipulations of oracles in the *Oresteia*.

53. But on the *symbolon*, which in its ambiguity and its union of contraries is essentially out of Clytemnestra's control, see Jean Lallot, "Xumbola kranai: Reflexions sur la fonction du *sumbolon* dans L'*Agamemnon* d'Eschyle," *Cahiers Internationals de Symbolisme* 26 (1974): 39–47.

54. For the definitive statement of this movement from female to male power in the *Oresteia*, see Froma Zeitlin, "The Dynamics of Misogyny: Myth and Mythmaking in the *Oresteia*," *Arethusa* 11 (1978): 149–84.

centerpiece of the *Oresteia*'s complex web of prophecy. In the *Choephoroe* Orestes relates Apollo's oracle that he will kill his father's murderers or pay the price with his own life (273–77). He asks, "Isn't it necessary to believe [or trust] [*pepoithenai*] such oracles?" (297). What exactly is meant by "believing" or "trusting" in the oracle is crucial here; commentators suggest that it means believing that Apollo supports the choice of killing the murderers.[55] In this sense, to "believe" or "trust" in the word of the god amounts to a belief in a divine authorization, or demand, for the action—which is exactly what is at stake in the *Eumenides*. But insofar as the oracle or *chrēsmos* here takes the form not of a prediction but, more characteristically, of a command, the formulation combines the act of belief with the act of obedience to Apollo. It is in this sense that the Areopagus's political affirmation of the "right" of Orestes' action in turn "fulfills" the oracle of Apollo, proving Apollo was "right." Aeschylus thus involves the civic court of Athens in ratifying Apollo's authority, which is essentially on trial in the final play.[56] Just as in *Agamemnon* the Chorus's acceptance of Clytemnestra's creation and interpretation of the sign confirms her political and symbolic power, here the political and dramatic confirmation of Apollo's oracle guarantees his authority, replacing Clytemnestra's—but only after it has been exposed as vulnerable.

The forms of the dramatic representation of prophecy are thus inseparable from the development of the political and social uses of prophecy, and more generally the ideas of political order and authority which prophecy represents. The authority of prophecy as a social phenomenon originates, certainly, in its association with divine inspiration; its power as language, however, lies in its polysemy, which both protects and undermines order. The power inherent in such polysemy is suggested

---

55. See the summary of readings of this line in Roberts, pp. 41–42.

56. See ll. 713–14, where Apollo asks the Chorus not to let his oracles be "fruitless" (*akarpotous*).

by the analogy between the function of ambiguity in oracles and that in jokes. According to Freud, "Nothing distinguishes jokes more clearly from all other psychical structures than this double-sidedness and this duplicity in speech."[57] Freud saw that in the same way that polysemous dreams subvert repression, jokes—particularly "tendentious" ones—"are especially favoured in order to make aggressiveness or criticism possible against persons in exalted positions who claim to exercise authority. The joke then represents a rebellion against that authority, a liberation from its pressure."[58] This "rebellion," of course, does not seriously threaten authority; jokes are a way to vent aggressiveness in terms of "play" rather than real revolution. In Greek tragedy the situation is reversed. Oracular polysemy is the mechanism used to assert and maintain established authority in the form of the image and voice of the god. No matter how the human questioner or consultant may try to prove the oracle "wrong," insofar as the oracle's words do not correspond directly to the "truth" or "facts" of the case, the multiplicity of meanings will always allow for the oracle to be "right." Greek history, however, provides many examples of the way humans manipulated the polysemy of oracles to get what they wanted.

Hegel construed the representation of oracular speech in tragedy as a sign of the gods' power; because they represent concrete universality, the gods in their universal wisdom naturally speak in equivocations, stating all sides of the truth. He saw that humans can select only one meaning of the words they speak in order to act, for action is necessarily definite and univocal. This necessity for action leads mortals inevitably into collision with the other voices or truths that "lay already folded in the oracular sentence."[59] In epic, humans, who must act, can

57. Sigmund Freud, *Jokes and Their Relation to the Unconscious*, trans. and ed. James Strachey (New York: Norton, 1960), p. 172.

58. Freud, p. 105.

59. *Hegel on Tragedy*, ed. A. and H. Paolucci (New York: Doubleday, 1962), p. 170.

recognize only one "truth," which they call right or wrong. When tragedy moves the hero into the context of the city, however, the problem of recognizing the truth becomes a political as well as an ethical issue, as men and women come into conflict over who has the right to speak the truth, and to speak for city or state.

CHAPTER 2

The Nature of Signs

The tradition of the tragic hero's defiance of prophecy begins, for us, in the *Iliad*, where mortals conflict and con-
spire with the gods in a struggle for a doomed city. Any
discussion of the tragic defiance of prophecy must begin with
Hector. His story, like so many stories in the *Iliad*, must have
served as a model for the Attic tragedians, who were devout
students of Homer. It represents both the beginning of the
literary tradition of the defiance of prophecy and an example
against which later versions can be tested.

It is Hector who defines this tradition of defiance rather than
Achilles, for Hector alone comes to doubt prophecy, while
Achilles always believes it. If, as Cedric Whitman says, Achilles
"is never deluded or willfully blind," Hector "behaves as
though he well might win."¹ Despite repeated warnings from
god and prophet, Hector recognizes his "fate" only when he
confronts death directly in his final battle with Achilles. Hector
does not react to prophecy as does Achilles, who both believes
the prophecies concerning his life and attempts to transcend

1. Cedric H. Whitman, *Homer and the Heroic Tradition* (Cambridge,
Mass.: Harvard University Press, 1958; rpt. New York: Norton, 1965), p.
208.

their limits. Rather, Hector challenges prophecy and remakes the prophetic sign to reflect his own values and will. In a sense, Achilles and Hector, separately, are the begetters of two lines of heroes: Achilles of heroes who strive to be gods—the "over-reachers" and "Herculean heroes"[2]—and Hector of heroes who experience exaltation and defeat solely on human terms—the line of Oedipus and Eteocles, Lear and Othello.[3] It is not just Hector's capacity for error that makes him the prototype for the tragic hero who defies prophecy; it is also his persistent assertion of heroic and communal values against the gods' predefinition. Hector misreads or cannot accept the gods' word when it conflicts with his own definition of *anankē*, even when that refusal of prophecy must lead him and his people into defeat.

Hector's deliberate misreading of the god-sent signs that foretell his doom serves as an important literary model for the political interpretation of omens. To the degree that we admire heroic subjectivity, we identify with a hero such as Hector when he defies supernatural authority, expressing his desire for autonomy. The corollary of this defiance, however, is the hero's desire to appropriate the power of signification for himself. In resisting prophecy, the hero exposes the conventional nature of the gods' language, trying to rob it of its magic and thus its authority. At the same time, the hero tries to supplant the gods' signs with his own "magic" and prodigious language, to in-

2. See Harry Levin, *The Overreacher* (Cambridge: Harvard University Press, 1952), and Eugene M. Waith, *The Herculean Hero in Marlowe, Chapman, Shakespeare and Dryden* (New York: Columbia University Press, 1962).

3. James Redfield, who reads the *Iliad* as the "tragedy of Hector," makes the difference clear: "Achilles is a strange, magical figure, with his immortal armor, his talking horses, and his sea-nymph mother, through whom his will has power even among the gods; Hector is a human creature, with wife and child, parents and brothers, friends and fellow citizens. Achilles' acts are always true to his shifting visions of himself; Hector has placed his life at the service of others. Between Hector and Achilles the outcome is never in doubt, for Achilles is superhuman, while Hector is only the sort of hero that we ourselves, at our moments of greatest aspiration, might hope to be." See *Nature and Culture in the "Iliad": The Tragedy of Hector* (Chicago: University of Chicago Press, 1975), p. 28.

fluence others and bring them to his cause; that is, the hero makes his own language seem the "natural" expression of human needs.

The battles between hero and prophet over the interpretation of signs, as first enacted in the *Iliad*, thus dramatize the argument about nature and convention, in language and society, as Plato later debated it. In *Cratylus*, playful as it is, Plato seriously investigates the role of power or control in signification. Hermogenes, arguing that naming is essentially conventional rather than natural, uses the example of the master's renaming of his slave. The newly imposed name is as correct as the old one, he says, because the slave will respond to it— for, indeed, as a slave he has no choice.[4] This model of convention thus implies that such naming or signification manifests an individual will with sufficient power to make and remake the signs of the world. Socrates, in turn, suggests that naming is instead "natural," that names are given "not according to our will" (*ouch hē[i] an hēmeis boulēthōmen*) but rather as they are "disposed by nature" (*hē[i] pephyke ta pragmata*).[5] In recounting a seemingly endless series of etymologies, Socrates argues for natural signification, maintaining that there is an "inherent" difference between truth and falsehood, which does not rely on individual judgments or will. Yet at the same time he insists that these "natural" names were given originally by the greatest of artisans, the lawgivers, and were thus indeed once imposed. In effect, Socrates here naturalizes his fundamentally political model of signification.

In the *Cratylus*, Plato in the end suggests a way in which convention can be identified with nature,[6] but in Callicles' ar-

4. *Cratylus* 384d.
5. *Cratylus* 387d.
6. See T. A. Sinclair, *A History of Greek Political Thought* (London: Routledge & Kegan Paul, 1951), on this aspect of Socrates' attitude toward the *nomos/physis* issue: "Socrates believed that it was in accordance with man's nature to act rightly, as soon as he knew what was right. If then we have laws, human laws, made so as to embody *to dikaion*, then *nomos* will no longer appear as an unnatural restraint on human conduct but as something in itself in accordance with nature" (p. 90).

gument in the *Gorgias*, he presents nature and convention at war once again. Here we encounter the nonlinguistic concept of convention as a code of rules agreed upon by a community, or more generally, as moral tradition and custom.[7] Socrates' antagonist, Callicles, the advocate of might as right, says that conventions are the rules made by men who are both weak and in the majority (*hoi polloi*),[8] but "natural men"[9] can overcome those rules, imposing their will on others.[10] Callicles claims that when we educate the young as we tame a wild beast, molding them to respect the laws and the values of equality and justice, it is as if we put them under a magic spell. But then there may come a man strong enough to shake off that spell, "trampling down our writings [*grammata*] and conjurations [*magganeumata*] and charms [*epō(i)das*] and laws, all against nature." Then "our slave in rebellion stands forth to be revealed as our master [*despotēs*], and there the light of natural justice is illumined."[11]

Here Callicles, like Hermogenes, suggests that convention is to be construed in terms of slavery and rebellion, mastery and weakness. Callicles envisions the man who rebels against slavery to convention as "natural" man, becoming our master, the tyrant, who rightfully enslaves us; thus "nature" becomes the new *nomos* or law.[12] In the rest of the dialogue Socrates undermines this idea, arguing that true happiness lies not in power but in goodness. But as Dodds suggests, in Callicles' speeches

7. See Ernest Barker, *Greek Political Theory: Plato and His Predecessors* (London: Methuen, 1918; rpt. 1961), p. 74.

8. *Gorgias* 483b

9. I use "natural men" to stand for the Greek *houtoi kata physin tēn tou dikaiou tauta prattousin*, "those who do things according to natural justice" (*Gorgias* 483e).

10. E. R. Dodds notes in his commentary on the *Gorgias* (Oxford: Clarendon, 1959): "Hitherto Callicles has used *nomos* in the sense of 'convention'; now he speaks of *hoi nomoi*, the laws of the state, thus tacitly equating law with convention" (p. 266).

11. *Gorgias* 483e–484a.

12. Sinclair, p. 77.

"we may feel the force of Plato's own reactions to democracy, though his practical conclusions were different."[13]

This rhetoric of power, associated with the representation of nature and convention, helps us to understand the contradictory nature of the hero's contest with the gods, for the hero sees the gods as imposing the meaning of his life through the spells of prophecy. At first, the hero exposes the *gods'* language as mere convention, to show that these signs are arbitrary or even meaningless rather than inherent in the "natural" order of things. The crisis comes when the hero does so to reveal *himself* as master, trampling down those writings and spells only to enforce his own. Hector, as we shall see, says that he cares nothing for birds, whether they come on the right or the left. He deliberately demystifies the divine sign, calling the prophet a fool, not a seer, and the bird only a bird. But Hector also offers his own *oiōnos*, or bird sign, which is not a true omen but a cultural generality. Having received the assent of the others for his cultural and heroic sign, he relies on the magic of his own speech to direct the future, against the gods' signs—and so leads his city into disaster.

In Book 12 of the *Iliad* Hector begins his engagement with prophecy with an interpretation of a bird sign. As the Trojans advance on the Achaians' wall, an eagle gripping a snake appears suddenly before them. When the writhing snake wounds the eagle, the eagle drops it and flies off screaming (195–209). Polydamas, Hector's best counselor, interprets this event as signifying that if the Trojans break through the Achaians' wall, they, like the eagle, will not return to Troy safely. Accordingly, Polydamas advises Hector not to fight the Achaians to their ships.

13. Dodds, p. 267. We might wonder, with Werner Jaeger and others, whether the force of Callicles' rhetoric against convention suggests that "in his own character Plato had so much of that unruly will to power as to find, and fight, part of himself in Callicles": *Paideia: The Ideals of Greek Culture*, Vol. 2, trans. Gilbert Highet (New York: Oxford University Press, 1943), p. 138. (For other scholars with the same opinion, see Dodds, p. 267.)

Polydamas speaks here with the voice of prophet and poet. His interpretation of this omen exemplifies the Homeric prophet's technique as an imitation of Homeric poetics. Polydamas begins his reading of this sign by recreating the first two lines of the narrator's description of a high-flying eagle, carrying a bloody snake (219–21, repeating 201–3). Then he "rewrites" the story's end, leaving out the description of the fight between the eagle and the snake and adding an ending in which the eagle cannot now return with the snake as food for its children. On the basis of this addition, Polydamas then introduces the terms of comparison with the Trojans' situation: as they saw

> . . . a high-flying eagle (*aietos hypsipetēs*) coming on the
>   left of the people,
> carrying in its talons a bloody, monstrous snake,
> still alive; but he let it drop before returning home,
> did not succeed in carrying it home to his children.
> So we, even if we break through the gates and walls of the
>   Achaians,
> with our great strength, and the Achaians give way,
> we will not make our way back from the ships in order;
> for we will leave many Trojans behind us, whom the
>   Achaians,
> defending their ships, will cut down with the bronze.
>
> [219–27]

Polydamas can be said here to imitate the Homeric poet in two ways: first, by repeating the actual words of the narrator's description, mimicking his voice, and second, by revising the story of the eagle and snake and putting it in a human context through analogy, which is the modality of the Homeric simile. Polydamas thus plays two roles at this point in the narrative: he acts as a participant in the action and as the *mantis*, "prophet," with the sight of the gods—and of the poet. Whereas elsewhere in the *Iliad* he takes a much more active and "heroic" role, here Polydamas allies himself with both the poet and the

gods against the hero and his code.[14] Perhaps any person could
see in this sign the truism that those who fight for their lives
fight with fury and would "predict" that the Trojans would
not return without injury if they crossed the ditch. Yet Polydamas, at the end of his speech, says that he speaks as would
a *theopropos* ("seer") "in whom the people believe" (228–29).

Hector angrily opposes Polydamas's interpretation and advice, despite Polydamas's claim to authority and despite the
apparent value of the sign itself. He says Polydamas must be
mad to advise him to trust in birds (234) instead of the promise
he believes Zeus has given him, "nodding in assent" (*kateneuse*,
236). Instead, he states his own creed:

> You bid me to trust in long-winged birds,
> which I neither care for nor heed,
> whether they come on the right by the dawn and sun,
> or on the left, by the misty realms of gloom.
> But we will trust in the counsel of great Zeus,
> who rules all mortals and immortals.
> One bird sign is best, to fight to defend your country
>
> [237–43]

Hector thus attacks Polydamas on four fronts: he challenges
Polydamas's capacity to prophesy, suggesting he is mad; he
dismisses the value of bird signs, saying they have no "natural"

14. Polydamas is not, of course, an "official" prophet, like Calchas or
Helenos, but he does assume, as other Homeric characters do, the privilege
of interpretation. Whitman describes him as one "who is not possessed by
princely presumptions but gifted with insight into omens" (p. 210). In most
cases, Hector willingly agrees with Polydamas's advice: see, for example, *Iliad*
12.60ff., 13.725ff. In 18.285ff., Hector disagrees with him, but he accepts
Polydamas's wisdom later in 22.100ff. It is interesting that Hector and Polydamas are said to have been born on the same night, the one born "greater
with words," the other "greater with the spear" (18.251–52). For an example
of an "official" prophet's interpretation of a bird sign, see Calchas's interpretation of the sign of the sparrow and snake, as related by Odysseus in
Iliad 2.322ff. For examples of bird-sign interpretation in the *Odyssey*, see
Halitherses' interpretation in *Odyssey* 2.146–207 and Helen's interpretation
in *Odyssey* 15.160–78.

significance; he offers his own reading of Zeus's *boulē* ("coun-sel" or "will"); and he proposes his own "bird sign" to supplant the gods' portent.

This scene demonstrates that Hector is willing to believe in omens only when he agrees with their meaning. He clearly devalues the significance of the bird sign by denying that it has any "magical" or divine significance. However, Hector's words, that he will trust the *boulē* of Zeus, recall Zeus's earlier sign to the Trojans in Book 8. There Hector boasts that Diomedes will never storm the battlements of Troy. Three times Diomedes ponders turning back, but Zeus thunders three times, as the narrator says, "making a sign [*sēma*] to the Trojans that victory in battle was changing sides" (171). Hector interprets this thunder as a sign that Zeus means for the Trojans to win the war. He says he knows that "kindly Zeus has nodded assent [*kateneuse*] to my victory and great glory, but suffering to the Danaans" (175–76). In the *Iliad*, typically, the divine sign appears for only a moment and then is erased—the thunder dies away or the bird disappears on the wind. Hector, however, takes Zeus's thunder, which signifies a temporary turn in the battle's tide, as an absolute affirmation of his boast that the Trojans will not conquer his city. He understands Zeus's prom-ise of favor as permanently inscribed, not just for the moment but for all time.

Hector refuses to accept Polydamas's interpretation and ad-vice not just because it contradicts his misreading of Zeus's will but also because it conflicts with his sense of his duty to defend his city. He therefore supplants Polydamas's reading with his own "ornithomancy": *heis oiōnos aristos amynesthai peri patrēs* (243), "one bird sign is best, to fight to defend your country." By shifting the denotation of *oiōnos* from "bird" or "bird sign" to the sign's content, he can offer as his *oiōnos* his belief in patriotic self-defense. Hector's reply to Polydamas thus represents not only a general lack of understanding of the divine sign's nature but also an impulse to replace the sacred with the secular, appropriating the power of the divine sign. To Hector, Polydamas is a fool rather than a seer, and the bird itself only a bird, no sacred omen, because in this case he chooses not to heed it (237). His substitution of a maxim for an *oiōnos* in line 243 climaxes this drive to rob Polydamas's words of any natural meaning and sacred authority. Hector offers as his *oiōnos* not an omen, divine and contextually specific, but a cultural generality.[15] Indeed, Hector succeeds, for the time being, in usurping the authority of Polydamas's reading of the bird sign. This success is evident in the troops' response to his speech, a triumphant shout, which is a formulaic response to a favorable omen: "Having spoken, he led the way and they followed with a divine cry" (*toi d'ham' heponto / ēchē[i] thespesiē[i]*, 251–52). At this moment, Hector's positive interpretation has effectively masked Polydamas's negative one, as the troops move to break down the wall, "trusting in the portents [*teraessi*] and their own strength" (256). Zeus himself participates ironically in the affirmation, sending a windstorm to magnify the Trojans' brief glory (253–55).

This scene in *Iliad* 12 is not the only example of Hector's persistent defiance of prophecies that conflict with his own vision of the future. In *Iliad* 13.810–37, when Ajax predicts that soon Hector will pray for his horses to carry him home swiftly, an *aietos hypsipetēs* ("high-flying eagle") appears on the right (cf. *Iliad* 12.200) in confirmation of Ajax's prophecy.

---

15. Wilamowitz and others have wondered at Hector's "incredulity." Yet Wilamowitz concludes that "this is not Euripidean skepticism, but something far better; the gods' and Polydamas' warning is entirely right, but it is the kind that a man with true heroic spirit throws to the wind." See U. von Wilamowitz-Moellendorff, *Die "Ilias" und Homer* (Berlin: Weidmannische Buchh., 1920), p. 217; translation mine. In his translation of the *Iliad*, Alexander Pope, too, notes that "there is something very heroic in that line: '— His Sword the brave Man draws / And asks no Omen but his Country's Cause.'" See *The Poems of Alexander Pope*, vol. 8, *The Translations*, ed. M. Mack, N. Callan, R. Fagles, W. Frost, and D. M. Knight (New Haven: Yale University Press, 1967), p. 91.

Hector does not openly acknowledge this omen;[16] he recognizes it only indirectly in his answer to Ajax, which closely parallels his reply to Polydamas in Book 12. He calls Ajax *hamartoepēs*, "missing the mark in his words," just as he accused Polydamas of madness. Further, his wish for divine kinship (824–27) corresponds, as an appeal to divinity, to his claim of Zeus's support in *Iliad* 12. Finally, he threatens Ajax with violent death and desecration of his body by dogs and birds, saying that "the Trojan dogs and birds [*oiōnous*] will feed on your fat and flesh, when you fall by the Achaian ships" (831–32). Once again, even as he makes an appeal to the divine, Hector transforms the divine sign into a secular one. Here he has translated the *oiōnos* (meaning "bird sign") that was a sign to the Achaians (823) into an *oiōnos* (meaning "bird") that will ravage the body of Ajax (831). Once more the Trojans take Hector's speech as a favorable sign, for the troops' response is expressed in the same formulas (*toi d'ham' heponto / ēchē[i] thespesie[i]*, 833–34) that follow Hector's reading of the bird sign in *Iliad* 12.251–52 (these are the only verses in Homer where these two formulas are conjoined). This conjunction of formulas juxtaposes the two occurrences of the *oiōnos*: its appearance to the Achaians as an omen and Hector's conversion of it into a scavenger bird, which the Trojans take as a portent of Ajax's death.

Insofar as the most immediate effect of Homeric omens is to encourage or dishearten the troops, Hector succeeds brilliantly in supplanting the divine sign by his own "magic" signs, his calls to courage. By the rules of the game, however, he cannot ultimately avert either the future events predicted by Polydamas or his own imminent death. The story is structured in such a way that it is his defiance that brings him to disaster.

---

16. Hildebrand Stockinger, in *Die Vorzeichen im Homerischen Epos: Ihre Typik und Ihre Bedeutung* (Tübingen, 1959), p. 134, notes that this lack of recognition of an omen is quite unusual in Homeric epic.

Yet even Hector's death itself evokes an *aietos hypsipetēs*—the third of the *Iliad*. In his last stand against Achilles (Book 22), when he knows Athena has tricked him, Hector realizes that he must die and that "so long before it must have been more pleasing to Zeus and Apollo, who yet defended me willingly before" (301–2). Yet he hopes even at this point that he may still seize *kleos* ("reknown") in the face of death. Even as he recognizes the inconsistency of divine favor, which he had not seen before in Zeus's signs, Hector springs to fight his enemy like another *aietos hypsipetēs*, diving out of the clouds to seize an innocent prey (306–10). Only here and in the two bird signs defied by Hector in Books 12 and 13 is the formula *aietos hypsipetēs* used in the *Iliad*;[17] when these passages are juxtaposed, Hector himself thus seems to become a bird sign, the omen of his own death. It is an ironic transformation, certainly, that Hector should become like the birds that were the messengers of his doom, but one can also say that, paradoxically, the simile affirms his control of signification. It is Hector's onslaught, his heroic action, that affords the interpretation of the sign; he fulfills it even as the poet speaks it.

Hector, indeed, has the last word in his conflict with prophecy before he succumbs to silence, when he not only demands a significance equal to that of the divine sign but also finds his own prophetic voice. Hector's final speech to Achilles foretells Achilles' own death, when the Trojan warns him to beware, lest Hector become a curse to him, "on that day when Paris and Apollo strike you down in the Skaian gates, noble as you are" (359–60). Hector tells Achilles not only that he must die soon, which the Greek hero already knows, but also where and at whose hands he will die. In a way reflecting the common superstition that "the soul at the moment of leaving the body

17. Menelaus and Achilles are also compared to an *aietos* in the *Iliad*, but not in this formula: Menelaus for his sight (17.674) and Achilles for his "spring" (21.252). But in the *Odyssey* the same formula is used to describe Odysseus's "last stand" (24.574–78).

was cognisant of the future,"[18] Hector discovers in his passage between the kingdoms of Priam and Hades a clear knowledge of what Achilles is now and what he will be. He thus resembles other Iliadic prophets in that he speaks outside of the *Iliad*'s temporal limits. But unlike them, Hector is not granted this privilege by the gods; no mention is made here of divine enlightenment. Rather, Hector seems to gain prophetic vision through the experience of dying. He does grant that in the end it is the divine pleasure, and not his own will, which has been fulfilled, yet he dies without seeking divinity. His final prophetic vision of Achilles' death does not come through his transcendence or elevation by the gods; rather, it comes in his own death—the one experience denied to the gods.

The power of Hector's example and its appeal to modern humanists lies, certainly, in his uncompromising claim for the primacy of human values in the face of the gods' amoral will and in the valorization of his death. Hector not only has the most significant death scene in the *Iliad*; he also is presented as a husband and father as well as a warrior, the opposite of angry Achilles. In Book 6, in his scene with Andromache and Astyanax, Hector recognizes and mourns that the day will come when Troy will be defeated and his wife led away a slave; yet he prays to Zeus that his son shall be a good fighter and live to outdo his father. In the same scene, when Andromache begs him to stay, he demonstrates this characteristic and contradictory mix of love and pride, fatalism and defiance. He says he cannot stay because he would feel shame before the Trojans if he did not fight, and in any case he is impelled to win great glory for himself and his father; yet he is also pained that

18. W. R. Halliday, *Greek Divination* (London: Macmillan, 1913), p. 202. Halliday continues: "The feeling seems to be that *in articulo mortis* the soul is on the borderland between the material and the spiritual worlds, and in the moment of crossing from one to the other is actually in touch with both. North Britons, indeed, have a word to denote the uncanny powers with which are credited those over whom death is imminent, and speak of the doomed and prescient as 'fey.' "

Andromache might live without him to protect her. He consoles his wife curiously, by saying that no man will kill him unless it is fated and yet reminding her that fate is inescapable. Hector never relents in opposing what must be and what should be.

Hector's descendants are the ethical and political heroes of later tragedy, the leaders of cities and states who suffer when they pursue a vision of self-determination and courage and see their people suffer. Unlike Achilles, Hector is the de facto leader of the Trojan people as well as of the Trojan warriors; once he is dead, everyone knows that the war, and Troy, are lost. Shakespeare's Troilus reminds us of that sense of an ending evoked by Hector's death: "Hector is dead," he says, "there is no more to say."[19] In Hector's role as leader we begin to see the ethical difficulties involved in his defiance of prophecy, which persist in the tragic versions of that defiance. Agamemnon's abuse of Calchas in Book 1 provides a revealing comparison with Hector's response to prophecy, clarifying Hector's success and failure as a leader of his people. When Calchas attributes the plague to Agamemnon's possession of Chryseis, Agamemnon at first turns against the prophet, accusing Calchas of always plotting against him. But in the end he agrees to give the girl back, in accordance with the prophet's advice (106–17). Agamemnon wishes that his "people would remain safe and not be destroyed" (117), and so he does what the prophet says. Indeed, Agamemnon does resist Calchas at first only because Calchas wants to take away his *geras* ("reward") and not because of any higher principle, whereas Hector seems to have a nobler motive, the desire to defend his country. Yet Agamemnon believes Calchas and responds to his request in an effort to end the plague and save his men, whereas Hector's defiance of Polydamas leads his men into the predicted disaster. Agamemnon challenges the prophet as a bringer of bad news, but not his prophecy; he yields to placate the gods, accepting

19. William Shakespeare, *The History of Troilus and Cressida*, 5.10.21–22, in *The Complete Works*, ed. Alfred Harbage (Baltimore: Penguin, 1969).

them on their own terms. Hector refuses to accept the gods' definition of necessity, but he sacrifices his troops to his own understanding of *ankē*, supplanting the gods' definition.

In his soliloquy in Book 22, as he awaits Achilles' approach, Hector admits that his tactical errors and rejection of Poly-damas's military advice have harmed his people, yet he holds fast to his defiance of prediction. In Book 18, after Achilles announces his return to battle, Polydamas advises Hector, for tactical reasons, to retreat within the city's walls, but Hector once again angrily rejects his counsel. Much later, after Achilles' bloody rout of the Trojans, Hector is left alone to consider his choices (22.99–107). At first he admits that his earlier disobedience of Polydamas has ruined his people, and he confesses his shame that someone might say that "Hector, believing in his own strength, destroyed his people" (107). Yet even as he recognizes Polydamas's wisdom, Hector speaks of military policy and not of fate; he never mentions or thinks with shame of Polydamas's augury. In the rest of the speech, what takes precedence is his defiance of Achilles, who, like the ominous Dog Star (22.29–32), is a sign of Hector's death and the manifestation of his fate. At first Hector contemplates talk-ing to Achilles and trying to strike a bargain, but then he suddenly decides that with Achilles, as with fate, there is no compromise, only conflict (22.122–30).

In the *Iliad* we are always reminded that Hector's defiance of Achilles and his fate is one small link in Zeus's plot to give Achilles glory, a plot that culminates in Hector's death. In this sense, from the gods' point of view, there is no conflict between the divine will and Hector's. Hector himself, however, until his death forces an opposition between the sacred plan and the heroic code. For him the gods' signs are significant only when they coincide with his own intentions and perceptions and his understanding of the heroic code. In Book 12, Hector fashions his own *oiōnos*, to which he attributes the authority and "magic" of a divine sign; in doing so, he creates a situation in which the divine and heroic words contradict each other, as if only one or the other could be true. The sign predicts disaster, and so Polydamas counsels retreat, but Hector refuses to recognize the possibility of disaster because for him it is "true" that he must fight to defend his country and thus advance, not retreat. What Hector discovers at last, facing Achilles in combat, is that his and the gods' signs are in fact two kinds of truth. True, the omen is fulfilled, and the Trojans are driven back from the ships at great cost, but in terms of the *Iliad*'s heroic norms, this outcome is not meant to invalidate Hector's *oiōnos*. The heroic code of the *Iliad* enforces the warrior's reponsibility to "fight among the foremost" and never retreat, and so Hector, dismissing retreat, acts within the heroic code. Further, it is true that Hector dies as the gods and prophet foretold, but it is his choice to die with *kleos*. The culture of the *Iliad* clearly establishes the importance of this choice, as Redfield describes it: "Man dies in any case, but he can choose to die well. He becomes a hero because he cannot be a god. In his nature the hero remains like other men, but culture bestows on him value; he does not survive, but he is remembered."[20]

What is left out of this formulation is the actual cost to the community of the hero's self-affirmation in acting according to the heroic code. The epic sets up the conflict in such a way that Troy must fall because Hector believes he should never retreat and because he must speak and act out that belief in defiance of prophecy. The questions that Hector and Agamemnon raise momentarily about what is best for the people are forgotten. Ultimately, from the hero's point of view, the role of the community is to perpetuate the hero's *kleos*, as the essence of *kleos* is their remembering and telling stories of the dead. The hero is envisioned as surviving after death in human speech, in the memories and voices of the generations to come.

20. Redfield, p. 101.

It is ironic indeed that Hector's actions in pursuit of *kleos* should bring about the destruction of the community that might preserve his heroism as its own story; Hector's story will belong to the Greeks.

CHAPTER 3

Speech and Authority: *Antigone*

As in the *Iliad*, in Sophocles' Theban plays mortals challenge the gods' definition of necessity in order to assert their own values. In Sophocles' plays, however, this confrontation takes place not on the battlefield but within the city of Thebes, where the tragic hero's claim to autonomy reflects the tyrant's arrogation of power. Each of these plays links the grasping for absolute power with the "heroic" response to the silence of oracular authority.

Greek tragedy, as a new genre, thus revised and reevaluated the epic model of heroic defiance according to the values of the Greek city-state. Gerald Else, in *The Origin and Early Form of Greek Tragedy*, argues convincingly that Greek tragedy, rather than originating as Dionysiac or cult ritual, was invented as a genre that would represent the epic hero in a civic context.[1] More recently John Herington has suggested a thematic and stylistic continuity between Greek tragedy and early Greek poetry, which strengthens our perceptions of tragedy's ties to early

1. Gerald Else, *The Origin and Early Form of Greek Tragedy*, Martin Classical Lectures, vol. 20 (Cambridge: Harvard University Press, 1965).

poetry as opposed to ritual.[2] Jean-Pierre Vernant explores the ideological implications of that continuity when he says that heroic and civic values clash when tragedy brings the heroes of the past into the very different world of the *polis*: "These heroes and heroic legends, while they are relegated to the past, condemned, called into doubt, still do not cease to stimulate certain questions, precisely insofar as they represent mental attitudes, values, patterns of behavior, a religious thought, a human ideal which is opposed to that of the City."[3] When Sophocles' protagonists challenge the gods' authority, they act out a heroic pattern of behavior which conflicts with the ideology of the Athenian city-state, especially with civic definitions of sacred and secular authority and civic equality. The Theban plays, *Antigone* in particular, thus set the defiance of prophecy in the context of a political crisis, so that the conflict between tragic fate and free will surfaces in the confrontation between citizen and tyrant, as the tyrant would silence the citizen. In *Oedipus the King*, Oedipus exposes the connection between the defiance of oracles and the desire for absolute political and personal autonomy. Having proven to be both criminal and despot, Oedipus is stripped of his kingship, yet he is established as a hero, who speaks in the face of the silent, implacable gods. It is only in *Oedipus at Colonus*, which moves outside the walls of Thebes to the sacred grove of Colonus (which was both part of and outside Athens), that a merging of political and divine authority is achieved, and Oedipus comes to speak as a prophet for Athens and Thebes alike.

Sophocles' earliest Theban play, *Antigone*, takes as its subject

2. John Herington, *Poetry into Drama: Early Tragedy and the Greek Poetic Tradition* (Berkeley: University of California Press, 1985). Herington reminds us, "The ancient critics agreed that [Sophocles] was *Homerikotatos*, the most Homeric of them all" (p. 137).

3. Jean-Pierre Vernant, "Greek Tragedy," in *The Structuralist Controversy: The Languages of Criticism and the Sciences of Man*, ed. Richard Macksey and Eugenio Donato (Baltimore: Johns Hopkins University Press, 1972), p. 283.

the instability of civic and religious authority, which is open to the threat of tyranny and anarchy alike. In the city of Thebes, Antigone defies the edict of Creon, the city's leader, who claims the priority of that edict over what Antigone calls the *agrapta nomima*, unwritten customs or traditions. The play's political crisis thus identifies the problem of authority with the issues of allegiance and identity; whom you obey in this city depends on who you think you are and how you define yourself in terms of family, city, or divinity.

A key moment in that political crisis is Creon's confrontation with the prophet. After Antigone has left the stage, lamenting her end, Tiresias appears, unsummoned, advising Creon to bury Polynices and free Antigone. Creon angrily rejects Tiresias's advice, and the prophet retaliates by predicting sure disaster for Creon and his family. After Tiresias exits, Creon decides, with the Chorus's help, to try to avert the prophesied ruin by suspending his punishment, but he comes too late to save Antigone and his despairing son. Like Hector, Creon does obtain a "prophetic" vision, but it is one ironically evoked by his son's wail of pain at Antigone's tomb. What Creon discovers "prophetically" is what Hector already knows: the inevitability of death and the necessity of love.

Many critics of the play have emphasized that Creon's actions mark his *lack* of heroic stature, even if they seem to resemble a "heroic" defiance of prophecy like Hector's. For most such critics, Creon's defiance cannot be heroic, if only because, for them, Antigone is so clearly the heroine of the play.[4] These readers generally dislike Creon, dismissing him as

---

4. James Hogan, in "The Protagonists of the *Antigone*," *Arethusa* 5 (1972): 93–100, while arguing that there is no *single* protagonist in the play, gives a good review of those who think Antigone—or Creon—the hero. See also William M. Calder III, "Sophokles' Political Tragedy, *Antigone*," *Greek, Roman, and Byzantine Studies* 9 (1968): 309–407, on Creon as the protagonist in the historical context of Athenian politics. Calder claims that "to side with Antigone implies an historical anachronism" (p. 404).

a "shallow" or "uninteresting" man,[5] while for others, Creon's abuse of Tiresias is unheroic because it is not complete.[6] My point is not to pronounce judgment on Creon's character or lack of it but to examine Sophocles' use of epic's model of the defiance of prophecy and the civic values associated with that defiance.

In *Antigone*, Sophocles uses Creon's opposition to Antigone to portray the tyrant's mimicking of the hero's role, when he claims the priority of communal values yet covets divine status.[7]

5. Only C. M. Bowra accepts Creon entirely as an Aristotelian hero, which he defines as a powerful man with a grave defect of character. See his *Sophoclean Tragedy* (Oxford: Clarendon, 1944), p. 102. But see also Robert Goheen, *The Imagery of Sophocles' "Antigone"* (Princeton: Princeton University Press, 1951), p. 98, and H. D. F. Kitto, *Greek Tragedy* (1939; rpt. Garden City, N.Y.: Doubleday, 1950), pp. 125–31, on the play as Creon's tragedy. A. J. A. Waldock, in *Sophocles the Dramatist* (Cambridge: Harvard University Press, 1951), says that Creon is "in essence, an uninteresting man, commonplace in all but his obstinacy" (p. 123). Cedric H. Whitman, in *Sophocles: A Study of Heroic Humanism* (Cambridge: Harvard University Press, 1951), too, finds Creon shallow: "There is nothing tragic or even morally interesting about him. Whether we find Creon thoroughly hateful or merely pitiable, his plight brings little satisfaction. He is puny" (p. 90). See also Brian Vickers, *Towards Greek Tragedy: Drama, Myth, Society* (London: Longman, 1973), pp. 526–46, and G. M. Kirkwood, *A Study of Sophoclean Drama* (Ithaca: Cornell University Press, 1958), p. 123.

6. Bernard Knox thinks Creon shows heroic "symptoms" until he yields, at last, to Tiresias's threats: "In Creon we are presented with the spectacle of a man who displays every symptom of heroic stubbornness, who is placed in the classic situation of the Sophoclean hero, expressed in the appropriate formulas, but who is swayed by advice, makes major concessions, and collapses ignominiously at the first real threat." For Knox, Creon's failure as a hero thus comes when he fails to sustain his defiance of Tiresias, giving in, at last, to his admonishments. See *The Heroic Temper: Studies in Sophoclean Tragedy* (Berkeley: University of California Press, 1964), p. 68.

7. It could be claimed that because of the play's conclusion, Creon's initial rejection of Tiresias is not like Hector's defiance at all, but merely a version of Agamemnon's abuse of and eventual capitulation to Calchas in Book 1 of the *Iliad*. Yet Creon's episode with Tiresias differs from Agamemnon's in an important respect: Agamemnon simply gives in to Calchas's advice about improving the present situation; Creon, however, while taking Tiresias's initial *advice*, believes that by his own actions he can keep the prophet's words from coming to fruition. Creon's actions resemble Hector's more than Agamemnon's, in that they express his resistence to "prediction."

In the beginning of the play, indeed, Creon would seem to be Thebes' Hector, devoted to the city's good and to secular values. From his first speech, Creon is portrayed as one who puts the concerns of city and man above all others.[8] Sophocles creates a situation, however, in which Creon, as the tyrant, asserting the priority of the human voice, subverts the communal values Antigone upholds.

In a traditional reading of the conflict in the play, *Antigone* may seem to reverse the terms of the epic defiance of prophecy. Here the "heroic" Antigone upholds the "divine law" while defying the king's secular proclamation, whereas Creon, her antagonist, rejects divine authority in favor of the city's interests. Yet in Sophocles' redefinition of the heroic pattern in an explicitly civic context, Creon's defense of the secular authority and the assertion of the truth of his own words become, in the course of the play, an imitation of the gods' unchallenged and inflexible authority. This "hero's" declaration of principles becomes the tyrant's fatal mandate. In many ways, Antigone and Creon are uncomfortably alike in this play: both are stubborn and cold and reject their kin in their effort to pursue what they think is right. More important, at times both seem to threaten the order and principles of the city. In effect, Sophocles reduplicates the pattern of the defiance of prophecy in both characters, and both endanger the city. Antigone comes to take the hero's role when she defies the "prediction" of Creon, who strives to become the city's new god, while Creon, as the "hero" who would defy the tyrannical gods, has become the tyrant himself. Just as the epic hero speaks out against the god's silent writing, Antigone speaks out against Creon's tyrannical imposition of silence and his "fatal" sentence of death.

Antigone asks the questions about truth and political right

8. As Victor Ehrenberg says in *Sophocles and Pericles* (Oxford: Blackwell, 1954), Creon seems to live "in a world where the gods have no say, a world of purely human and political standards" (p. 54), while Antigone, (whatever her motivation for disobeying Creon) seems to most readers to be "the voice of obedience to the eternal divine laws" (p. 31).

implied by the conflict between hero and prophet in the *Iliad*: Do god and prophet always speak the truth? Is the *tyrannos* always right, simply because he rules? Or is the truth to be found instead in the consensus or common experience of all men and women? Such questions lie at the root of the play's manifold contests for the right to say what is necessary and lawful. In this century, most scholars of *Antigone* have resisted the Hegelian reading of the play as a conflict "between the family right and state right [in which] neither can be said to be wrong or entirely justified."[9] Critics such as Bowra, Reinhardt, Vickers and Whitman, who focus on character portrayal, think that the play shows us clearly who is right—Antigone— and who is wrong—Creon.[10] But in terms of the politics of the play, rather than the personalities, the conflict of rights remains complex. If authority is assigned solely by hierarchy, Creon can be both right and wrong: he has authority within the *polis* as the city's chosen leader, and yet he apparently threatens the hierarchical order of mortals and gods by claiming the priority of the city's needs over the gods'. If we consider political right in terms of a mid-fifth-century standard of political *aretē*, "the belief that any individual potentially contains valid insight into justice, divine and political,"[11] insofar as she is regarded as a citizen, Antigone might have equal authority to speak in the city. Yet, in fifth-century Athens, Antigone, as a woman, would not have the right to speak in a public forum at all, and Creon never tires of reminding us that she is a woman.

Marcel Detienne has proposed a model for the social determination of *alētheia* ("truth") which is useful in understanding

9. Whitman, p. 84: "This interpretation was at first followed implicitly, and later gave rise to different but equally schematized views: that Antigone represents 'magnanimity' and Creon 'self-restraint,' or that the play shows the conflict between religion and the state." Cf. *Hegel on Tragedy*, ed. Anne Paolucci and Henry Paolucci (New York: Harper & Row, 1962), pp. 73–74.

10. Bowra, pp. 66–67; Whitman, p. 85; Vickers, pp. 542–43; and Karl Reinhardt, *Sophocles*, trans. H. Harvey and D. Harvey (1947; rpt. New York: Barnes & Noble, 1979), p. 65.

11. Whitman, p. 87.

this problem of authority and speech in *Antigone*.[12] Detienne speculates that in its "prehistory" the declaration of *alētheia* was the *function* of prophet, poet, and king; in their voices, truth was asserted, not proved. In a society in which *alētheia*, like law, is thus instituted ritually, "truth is not the agreement of a proposition with its object, nor the agreement of a judgment with other judgments"; rather, truth is what prophet, poet, or king says has been, is, or will be.[13] Detienne hypothesizes further that historically the category of *alētheia* changed according to modifications in the social structure. With the "laicization" of society came the laicization of *alētheia*: as the *logos* became common property, *alētheia* was no longer defined by its source, but by communal assent and empirical verification.[14]

Even if such an original, ritual discourse was only a fiction, Detienne's model of the "history" of *alētheia* illuminates the conjunction of political and ideological conflicts in *Antigone*. In Detienne's terms, Sophocles depicts a situation in which the privilege to declare law, and implicitly to declare the truth, is claimed by a "king." Yet this is a society in which each citizen, too, possesses the *logos*. In asserting the priority of his *kērygma* or "proclamation," over all other statements (as if he were a god or prophet proclaiming *anankē*), Creon claims that what he, the leader, says, must *be*. But he does not go unchallenged in the context of the *polis*.

Thus what the play offers is a kind of "double exposure" of political systems: we see Creon claiming his rights as king to speak the truth for the city in a society that stresses the communal and empirical definition of *alētheia*. The play's placement of the figure of the king in a city that resembles the contemporary Athenian *polis* may also be seen as a version of what Vernant describes as tragedy's representation of heroic

12. Marcel Detienne, *Les Maîtres de la vérité dans la Grèce archaïque* (Paris: Maspero, 1967).
13. Detienne, p. 27.
14. Detienne, ch. 5.

values in a civic context. Even as Athens wants the old heroes of myth, it must reject them, or redefine them, insofar as "the ideal of the City is for citizens to be equal, whereas the heroic ideal is to be always first."[15] Historically, the situation also reflects the precariousness of Athenian democracy, which was always endangered by the threat of a demagogue's seizure of power.

Creon's attempt to be "first" in Thebes is expressed primarily through his efforts to control speech. His reaction to the prophet is not an isolated incident, but the climax of his effort to speak with a king's voice, and eventually with the voice of a god. The focus of *Antigone*'s conflict is Creon's insistence on the priority of his *kērygma* forbidding the burial of Polynices. Basic to Creon's fear of not being obeyed in this crisis is his fear that his *kērygma* forbidding Polynices' burial will not be believed. To reverse his position on Antigone's punishment, he says, would be to prove himself a liar, since he has declared that the disobedient will be punished (655–58). He does not, of course, admit that he might be wrong or that his word could be taken back. Creon complains that Antigone boasts and laughs about what she has done (483),[16] thus suggesting that Antigone's disregard of his *kērygma* is not simply disobedience but a response that devalues and contradicts his very words (the verb *apisteuō* used in l. 656, *poleōs apistēsasan ek pasēs monēn*, means both "disbelieve" and "disobey").[17] In the course of the play Creon thus tries to make us believe that he speaks a language different from Antigone's and ours. His lan-

15. Vernant, p. 283. For the political "anachronisms" of Greek tragedy, see Anthony J. Podlecki, "Polis and Monarch in Early Attic Tragedy," in *Greek Tragedy and Political Theory*, ed. J. Peter Euben (Berkeley: University of California Press, 1986), pp. 76–100.

16. As Charles Segal observes, "for Creon, Antigone's *hybris* or outrage of public order lies not only in having done the deed but in her manner of communicating it": *Tragedy and Civilization: An Interpretation of Sophocles* (Cambridge: Harvard University Press, 1981), p. 163.

17. Cf. also ll. 219 and 381. While *apisteuō* clearly denotes "disobedience," the second sense of "disbelief" undercuts Creon's pretense of authority.

guage is public, performative, and impersonal; hers, single and private. He is identified as the city's representative; she is alone, with only the gods as her witnesses. (Throughout the early episodes of the play, Ismene, Creon, and the Chorus all call her *monē*, "alone".)

Indeed, at the beginning of the play it appears that Creon and Antigone do exist in different worlds and speak different languages. As the prologue shows Antigone taking Ismene aside, that she may hear the news of Creon's public proclamation alone (*hōs monē klyois*, 19), Antigone seems to oppose her single voice against Creon's official one and the voice of public rumor. Indeed, when Creon first appears with the Chorus, identified as the council of elders of Thebes, he declares his platform as a leader,[18] which would establish his position as the city's defender. Creon seems the supreme "Periclean" man in this speech, ready to sacrifice all for the public welfare, unlike Antigone, who seems compelled only by her own desires.

As the play progresses, however, it appears that this opposition between Antigone and Creon is not so clear-cut. Despite the punishment of perpetual solitary confinement decreed by Creon,[19] Antigone is seen, in fact, not to be alone; she does not remain in private, although she must act alone. Creon says he condemns Antigone to lingering death in isolation to avoid the defilement (*miasma*) of the city which would be incurred by execution within its walls (776). What he really fears, though, is her ability to contaminate the citizens' opinions. At the beginning, when her sister Ismene begs Antigone to keep her disobedience a secret, Antigone angrily retorts that it must be made public. If you do not tell the world *my kērygma* (*kēryxe[i]s tade*, 87), she says, I will hate you. What Antigone wants is to respond to Creon with a contradictory decree; she fights back not by opposing her private needs to his public necessity but on his own level, in public.

18. See Ehrenberg, p. 58
19. *Antigone* 771–80.

Antigone devalues Creon's *kērygma* further, saying ironically that for her it does not supersede the necessity of burial, for Zeus made no such *kērygma* to her (*kēryxas tade*, 450). She sets against Creon's word the *agrapta nomima*, where *agrapta* means "unwritten" and *nomima* signifies not exactly laws but traditional customs shared by the community or ritual practices that have the force of law.[20] When Antigone reminds Creon that neither Zeus nor Dikē made such a decree against burying Polynices, she is not insisting, certainly, that only the gods can make laws. What she says is that Creon's decree does not have the force to revoke the long-established tradition of burying the dead. Here Antigone appears to defend human custom, which is invested with the authority of tradition. She sets Creon up as the one who would rise above that kind of law, and calls upon the citizens—Creon's citizens—to bear witness: "They would speak," she claims before Creon, "if fear did not lock up their tongues" (505). Creon retorts "You alone [*mounē*] of the Cadmeans see it that way" (508), but Antigone insists that they see it her way, but do not speak for fear of offending their leader. At this point it becomes clear that Thebes is a city where any public speaker needs the citizens' assent, as both Creon and Antigone are concerned about the citizens' opinions. Antigone presents her case not simply as an individual but also as a communal cause, while Creon attacks Antigone because she differs from the rest of the citizens (510)—who themselves remain silent.

It is all the more surprising, then, that in the episode that follows, in which Haemon accuses Creon of the very singularity he attributed to Antigone, Creon denies his need for the city's

20. See Knox, *Heroic Temper*, in a discussion of *Antigone* 449–55: "She is not opposing a whole set of unwritten laws to the written laws of the *polis*, nor is she pleading the force of individual conscience or universal and natural law. She is claiming that the age-old customary rites of mourning and burial for the dead, which are unwritten because they existed even before the alphabet was invented or the *polis* organized, have the force of law, unwritten but unfailing, which stems from the gods and which the gods enforce" (p. 97). But see Ehrenberg, p. 31, for the opposite view on the significance of Antigone's stand on the *agrapta nomima*.

support. Haemon echoes what Antigone said, that the voice of the city is for Antigone and is repressed only for fear of Creon's reprisal: "Such is the rumor (*phatis*) that spreads in silence and darkness" (700). He says his father is the one who is alone (*hen ēthos mounon*, 705).

But Creon reacts to Haemon's admonishment not by denying that he is alone but by dismissing the supposition that he needs the city at all (736–39). He asks his son angrily, "Should I rule this land for others or for myself?" When Haemon replies that the city does not belong to any one man, Creon retorts that by law it belongs to him (738). Just as Creon condemns Antigone to suffer entombment in the wilderness (*erēmos stibos*, 773), so Haemon tells Creon that he should be king alone (*monon*) in a deserted land (*erēmes gēs*, 739).[21] At first Creon appeared as the city's legitimate representative, invested with the power to make *kērygmata*. When he refuses to reverse or contradict his *kērygma*, it is implied that he identifies his speech with his authority in the city. Yet as Antigone and Haemon begin to make him doubt the city's support for his words, Creon reacts by rejecting his city, representing his power as personal and inherent, rather than derived from the assent of others.

It is at this moment that Creon is revealed as a tyrant.[22] He is not a tyrant according to the terms of the traditional Platonic definition, for he has not committed moral crimes (although curiously Tiresias later will accuse him of a tyrant's greed).[23]

21. As Knox says, "Creon no longer speaks and acts for the *polis* as a whole; he speaks for no one but himself" (*Heroic Temper*, p. 108). See also Bowra, p. 103: "He falls into the tyrant's common fault of shutting himself off from other men, like Deioces, who established the rule that a king should see no one, or Pausanius, who when his head was turned by success, made himself inaccessible."

22. See Anthony J. Podlecki, "Creon and Herodotus," *Transactions of the American Philological Association* 97 (1966): 359–71, on Creon's becoming a tyrant.

23. For Plato on tyranny, see *Republic* 8. See also Herodotus, 3.80. On the subject of Greek tyranny, see Claude Mossé, *La Tyrannie dans la Grèce antique* (Paris: Presses Universitaires de France, 1969); and on the representation of tyranny in Greek drama, see Diego Lanza, *Il tiranno e il suo pubblico* (Torino: Einaudi, 1977).

Rather, he is tyrannical in his belief in the power of his own voice and his separation of himself from the claims of humanity. In speaking, he is thus like the Syracusan tyrants Hieron and Gelon, who, as it is reported in a late anecdote, "indulged their savagery to the extent of forbidding the Syracusans to utter any sound at all, but to signify what was appropriate by means of their feet, hands, and eyes whenever one of them was in need." As Vincent Farenga comments, "the anecdote represents what for Gelon and Hieron would be the dream of a perfect tyranny: to stand above a silent city, hearing themselves speak but none other, hearing nothing, in fact, but the echo of their own voice."[24] Creon, too, wishes to set himself above and separate from the city, with unchallenged possession of the *logos*. In this play, where the claims of the city and gods first seem opposed, Sophocles presents Creon's fault not as the threat of an entirely secular rule, but as his attempt to claim that his voice is godlike, impersonal, and absolute, needing neither assent nor verification. Like the gods who speak through their prophets, Creon refuses to engage in dialogue or rescind his word—until it is too late.[25]

It is in this respect, then, that Sophocles casts Antigone's defiance of Creon as a political version of the epic hero's defiance of the prophet; that is, she defies a man who sets himself up as the master of her "fate." Just as it has been said that fate is recognized as external or compelling only when one person defies it, so Creon is seen to be a tyrant who speaks the "sentence" of death only in the face of Antigone's opposition. Some may say that Antigone defies Creon only in defense of a higher authority, in championship of the gods' supremacy, yet she does what she does to uphold the *nomima* and because she

---

24. Anecdote in Hugo Rabe, ed., *Prolegomenōn sylloge* (Leipzig: Teubner, 1931), pp. 24–25, n.4, as cited in Vincent Farenga, "Periphrasis and the Origin of Rhetoric," *MLN* 94 (1979): 1035, 1037.

25. As Gilberte Ronnet says, in *Sophocle: Poète tragique* (Paris: Boccard, 1969), "he has taken on the savage and inexorable mask that one usually attributes to fate" (p. 188; translation mine).

feels a duty to another human being, her brother. That much-contested speech[26] in which she asserts the priority of her duty to her brother over that to husband or child betrays her obsession with the sanctity of the relationships between kin (*kasignētoi*), which can never be replicated or violated (911–15). The expression of this obsession involves a contradiction typical of her character: in this speech Antigone signals her duty to Polynices through a denial of husband or child (a denial appropriate to a virgin), just as elsewhere she cuts herself off from her living sister; at the same time, however, she dreams of joining her cursed family in Hades.[27] But Sophocles intends her actions connecting herself with her kin, her fulfillment of her duty to brother and parents, to contrast with those of Creon, who in his tyranny completely cuts the bonds with both city and family; he prefers to stand alone, autonomous, a rival and imitator of the gods.

In the city of Thebes, Creon can play a god, as long as the gods themselves keep silent. At least one reader has seen Creon's fault to be his subversiveness, his "exalting the city above the gods and their laws, thus subverting the hierarchical order,"[28] but Creon obsessively maintains the social hierarchy, in particular the subjection of woman to man, son to father, and subject to king.[29] He wants less to subvert the order of god and mortal than to support the hierarchy in which he holds supreme authority. Up to the end of his episode with Haemon,

26. Many would like to delete this passage (904–20) from the play. See, e.g., Whitman, pp. 92–93, who follows Sir Richard Jebb, *Antigone*, app. 258ff., in *Sophocles: Plays and Fragments* (Cambridge: Cambridge University Press, 1928).

27. Knox, *Heroic Temper*, p. 107.

28. Gerald Else, *The Madness of Antigone*, Abhandlungen der Heidelberger Akademie der Wissenschaften: Philos.-Histor.-Klass. Abhandlungen, pt. 1 (Heidelberg: Carl Winter, 1976), p. 12.

29. For evidence of Creon's belief in patriarchy, see *Antigone*, 639–40, where he reminds Haemon that in all matters Haemon should submit his *gnōmē* ("opinion) to his father's will; also note Creon's insistence on the necessity of the subject's obedience to the leader (659–71) and his fear of submitting to a woman (525).

Creon confronts no person with power equal to his own. Then, at last, Creon faces Tiresias, the prophet of Apollo.

Tiresias's appearance in this play is the earliest in extant Greek tragedy.[30] He does play a part in *Odyssey* 11, telling Odysseus in Hades of his trials to come, as well as in Pindar's first Nemean ode. In the new papyri of Stesichorus's *Thebaïs* we see him associated with the house of Laius, prophesying about Eteocles and Polynices in Jocasta's presence.[31] In the *Odyssey*, as in Pindar's ode, Tiresias's role is that of an underworld prophet and revered interpreter; in *Antigone* he is presented in the context of the city, where he has a double function. On the one hand, he resembles the *Iliad*'s prophets, acting as the king's chief adviser, gifted with a special knowledge; on the other hand, he is identified as the sacred seer, inspired with the truth of Apollo and answerable to him alone.

Creon's scene with Tiresias falls into two parts, reflecting Tiresias's double role. In the first, Tiresias serves an essentially secular function, but in the second he evokes his sacred powers. Tiresias comes initially to give Creon advice about the present situation in Thebes, not to deliver any kind of prediction about the future. Like Polydamas, he bases his understanding of the present crisis and his advice for improving it both on his skill in reading ornithomantic and sacrificial signs and on his insight into human nature, reflected in the maxims at the end of his first speech. It is only when Creon rejects his advice that he shifts into the role of inspired or possessed medium of Apollo, threatening Creon with inevitable doom.[32] Tiresias's double

30. Tiresias appears later in Sophocles' *Oedipus the King* and in Euripides' *Bacchae* and *Phoenissae*. He is also alluded to, but not named, in Aeschylus's *Seven Against Thebes*, 24–29. See William Owen, "Teiresias: A Study in Dramatic Tradition and Innovation," Ph.D. diss., Princeton University, 1963.

31. See P. J. Parsons, "The Lille 'Stesichorus,' " *Zeitschrift für Papyrologie und Epigraphik* 26 (1977): 7–36.

32. It is generally accepted that the Greeks considered inspired or intuitive divination as more trustworthy than inductive divination, the former being "directly inspired by the god." See Robert Flacelière, *Greek Oracles* (New York: Norton, 1961).

role, as counselor and seer, thus challenges and destabilizes Creon's rigid hierarchy of authority. As secular adviser or adjunct to the king, Tiresias should be subject to Creon's civic authority, yet he also escapes the civic hierarchy by calling himself a servant of Apollo, not of Creon. Further, in terms of the system in which Creon claims his rights "by position," Tiresias has an equivalent claim that what he says must be: in the same system of thought that makes *alētheia* a function of the king's voice, Tiresias also has a traditional claim to speak the truth for the city.[33]

When Tiresias appears, he comes unsummoned; he wishes to advise Creon, as he has done in the past (991–94) for the benefit of the city, where sacred and secular interests are naturally allied. Just as Tiresias himself submits to the guidance of the sighted as he enters (989–90), so the state should now see with the prophet's eyes. The first mark of resemblance to the defiance of prophecy in epic poetry occurs in Tiresias's report of bird signs. In this case, however, the birds had come babbling (1001–2) and fighting murderously to where the prophet sat in his ancient augural seat (999). This bird sign signifies, paradoxically, a crisis in which signs fail: the voices of the birds themselves were unintelligible, even to the prophet, and their actions can only suggest violent disorder. Tiresias goes on to report that when he turned to sacrifice to discover the bird sign's meaning, the sacrifice, too, failed, for the offering would not burn. Such omens, he says, he has learned from the boy's report of the wasted rites (*orgia*), which are said to be *asēma*, "obscure" or "nonsignifying" (1012–13). These

---

33. Like the king and poet, the prophet should exercise a ritual power to declare the truth, a privilege granted not only by the community but also by the gods themselves. Marcel Detienne speculates that behind the mythic figuration of kings such as Minos and Nereus lies a figure that combines "royal function, justice, prophetic knowledge, and the privilege of *alētheia*" (p. 49). *Antigone*, like *Oedipus the King*, demystifies this figure, portraying a society in which king and prophet each claim the right to speak the truth. Both Creon and Tiresias speak of a past when they agreed on civic matters (991–94), but the play depicts a present in which they conflict.

omens are symptoms of a terrible silence, the very silence that
Creon would impose upon the city.

Tiresias can understand the actions of the birds and the
failure of sacrifice to mean only that Creon has interfered with
the relations between gods and mortals by allowing the public
altars to be contaminated by Polynices' flesh. He does not,
significantly, predict the future, but only offers a diagnosis of
Thebes' disease. In Tiresias's reading, Creon has, in effect,
blocked all communication between gods and mortals, so that
the gods, in turn, are silent, like Creon's constrained subjects.
The gods, however, not only do not communicate their will to
human beings but will not receive their sacrificial prayers
(1019). The crisis becomes grotesquely physical in Tiresias's
account: the altars of the city are covered with the decaying
flesh dropped by the scavenger birds and dogs, and "no bird
shrieks forth a cry of good omen [*oud'ornis eusēmous apor-
roibdei boas*], having gorged on the bloody flesh of the mur-
dered man"(1021–22).[34] What Creon has done, in fact, is to
produce what Hector predicted to Ajax in *Iliad* 13—the conversion of the gods' bird sign into a bird of prey. Creon has
created a crisis in which birds of omen become merely scavenger
birds, gorged with human flesh. Reflecting this crisis, Tiresias's
own concluding words in his first major speech emphasize secular wisdom rather than sacred knowledge. After concluding
his diagnosis of Thebes' disease, Tiresias advises Creon to cure
it quickly by yielding to the pleas of Antigone and others and
allowing the burial of Polynices. The prophet gives this advice
without referring to any supernatural mandate or insight. Instead, he calls himself simply a "good adviser" (*eu soi phro-
nēsas eu legō*, 1031) and offers Creon redemption in the
essentially secular world Creon claims as his own.[35] He reminds

34. Dawe deletes l.1021 as well as 1013, but I am not convinced that they
should be deleted; see Hugh Lloyd-Jones's review in *Classical Review* n.s. 31
(1981): 169–70.

35. As Knox says, here Tiresias makes "an appeal to reason, couched in
the classic formulas" (*Heroic Temper*, p. 73).

Creon that the king, like all humans, is fallible, but the prophet reassures Creon that he lives in a world where amends can be made (1023–27).

This first part of Creon's scene with Tiresias thus replicates the first step of Hector's defiance of prophecy, insofar as the divine sign is secularized and the prophet's advice rejected. In effect, the divine sign has already been demystified, but Creon takes things a step further. First, in his violent rejection of Tiresias, after Tiresias's plea for reason, Creon makes no mention of the bird signs or sacrifice; he does, however, say that the body must remain unburied, even if the eagles of Zeus carry the rotten flesh up to the gods (1040–41), so that the eagles who are messengers of the gods become the very real carrion birds who prey on the dead. Second, implicit in everything Creon says is the devaluation of Tiresias's words into common discourse. In *Iliad* 12, Hector attacks Polydamas first by suggesting that he is "wandering in his wits"; Creon, picking up on Tiresias's last word, *kerdos* ("gain" or "profit"), accuses Tiresias of being a kind of *chrēsmologos*, or trafficker in politically convenient prophecies (1034–36). To Creon, Tiresias's words have no real value because he believes they can be "exchanged" for money (reflecting Creon's obsession with the idea that the truth can be bought and sold, shown most acutely in his first scene with the sentry, 280–331).[36] In his rage, Creon accuses the prophet of dealing in the "common currency" of discourse (*poion touto pagkoinon legeis*, 1049); to him, Tiresias's advice is base coinage. Yet while he persistently secularizes Tiresias's words and position, Creon's inflexibility in response to Tiresias's plea for reason betrays his self-identification with divinity rather than humanity. The *Iliad* depicts a world in which the gods are inconsistent and placable, while the *moira* of mortals is forever fixed. Hector responds to these conditions with his own stubborn belief in human necessity. In *Antigone*, however, the gods and fate are fused together into

36. See Robert Goheen, pp. 14–19, on the "money sequence" of images.

one implacable force. Here Creon's stubbornness is evoked by Tiresias's plea that he see himself as human, fallible, and vulnerable in a human world of reason and pity.

Only when Creon and Tiresias reach this impasse does the second phase of the conflict begin. Tiresias shifts out of his role as the king's adviser and begins to speak as the inspired prophet. At first, he counseled according to his reason, but now, he says, Creon will drive him "to speak out what is inviolable [*taki-nēta*]" (1060). Tiresias' second speech makes no reference to deduction from signs, nor does it draw on common wisdom. Rather, it reveals a vision of Creon's future: in not many days, he says, Creon will give up one from his own loins in return for his burying Antigone alive and his refusal to bury Polynices (1066–67). Tiresias does not generalize he did before. The horror of his prediction comes from its specificity; he predicts the exact punishment for Creon's crimes. This prediction may be said to represent the "truth" in two ways: first, as it draws on the justice of equal retribution or exchange (ironically echoing Creon's economic obsessions) and second, as it goes beyond general wisdom in predicting the imminence of Creon's punishment, which only the prophet can know. Further, Tiresias's speech also shifts the crisis from the present to the future tense. While in his first speech Tiresias refers only to the present situation, in the second speech he says what the future will be, inexorably. He claims that once he has spoken the word of fate, "like an arrow loosed," its blow cannot be avoided (1084–86). In effect, he implies that the inflexible Creon has chosen an inflexible fate by rejecting the prophet's plea to relent in his stubbornness.

At this point, it is surprising that Creon and the Chorus still think a choice can be made, even as they attest that Tiresias has never yet lied to the city (1094). As Creon says, to yield is a terrible thing, but to dash his pride in ruin is worse (1096–97). Frightened by Tiresias's words, Creon turns to the Chorus for advice, saying that he will do as they say (1099). When they counsel him to free Antigone and bury Polynices, he chooses to give in and obey them, for "you fight a losing battle with necessity [*anagkē(i)*]" (1106). Most commentators describe this scene as the crisis of Creon's heroic career, in which he yields to Tiresias's superior authority and recognizes the irreversible will of the gods.[37] Other critics, however, note that Creon never does surrender his willfulness and his belief that events remain under his control.[38] Even as he prepares to undo his wrong, acknowledging that he "fears that it is best to keep the established laws [*tous kathestōtas nomous*] until we die" (1113–14), his words express his strong sense of his own will and power. He urgently orders the others to heed his commands to rescue Antigone, emphasizing his own responsibility and control: "I, in my good judgment, have now come around to this. I myself bound her, and I will set her free" (1111–12). Creon thus persists in believing that control of action and its consequences lies in his hands, even as he responds to his fear of uncontrollable ruin: he has created the disaster, he thinks, and he will be the one to remedy it. If the audience accepts Tiresias's words as irrevocable, however, they will see Creon as Reinhardt does when he observes that "his closing words when he at last decides to make haste only reveal again how deluded he is in his belief that human will can 'set free what it has bound.' "[39]

Why is it that we praise other heroes, in other stories, who

37. See Kirkwood, p. 124. See also Knox, *Heroic Temper*, pp. 67–68, and Whitman, who puts the emphasis somewhat differently: "But nothing new has happened, except that Creon is now able to look into a mirror large and authoritative enough so that even he cannot mistake the fatal outline of his own deed and the justice of Antigone's" (p. 95).

38. Bowra, p. 100, notes that "his conversion is only skin deep. He has as yet no regret, no sense of guilt. What impresses him is force of circumstance" (p. 100). Ronnet, too, sees that Creon does not "repent" here but only gives way because he is afraid and wants to avoid the consequences of his act (pp. 91–92).

39. Reinhardt, p. 91. Cf. Walter Jens, "Antigone-Interpretationen," in *Sophokles: Wege der Forschung*, vol. 95 (Darmstadt: Wissenchaftliche Buchgesellschaft, 1967): "He still believes that he need only take back his command and the order of things will be reestablished" (p. 310; translation mine).

are thus "deluded," and yet so many condemn Creon's delusion? One answer is that Sophocles, by identifying Creon's "heroism" with tyranny, explicitly politicizes his rejection of prophecy. Unlike Hector, who does not believe Polydamas's prophecy because he believes first in the values of his people, Creon is impelled to act on his own authority, not just because he believes Tiresias's words enough to be frightened by them but also because, as a tyrant, he is driven to dominate others. Creon is clearly acting in his own interests and in defense of his position throughout, even when he appears to give in to the prophet.

The final movement of the play, which consists of the Messenger's speech and Creon's return to Thebes with Haemon's body, completes the ironic parallel between Hector's and Creon's experience. The Messenger tells the Chorus and Eurydice how he guided Creon to the place where Polynices lay. When they had completed the duty of burial, they heard from the direction of Antigone's tomb the sound of a wailing voice, an ominous sound to Creon: the cry is said to be *asēma*, "inscrutable" or "unintelligible" (1209). Like Tiresias in his augural seat, Creon finds himself striving to interpret a sign or *sēma* which is *asēmon*, as were the cries of the birds that haunted the prophet. Horrified, Creon responds by recognizing his own position, which is analogous to Hector's in his last moments: "Oh, misery; am I the prophet [*mantis*] now?" (1212). Haemon's voice becomes the *sēma asēmon* of death, and Creon is the only seer who can interpret the sign—the father who can hear the agony in his son's voice. The *sēma asēmon* of Haemon's voice, reduplicating the violent bird cries, also marks Creon's disruption of all significant structures. Like the failed signs that Tiresias observed, which signaled the disruption of communication between gods and mortals, the voice of Haemon signifies a crisis of communication which has penetrated the family. By rejecting Haemon, Creon has ruptured the ties between father and son; it is due to Creon's violence that Haemon's voice, distorted with pain, is barely recognizable. Further, that Haemon's voice serves as a "sign" to this "prophet," his father, ironically fulfills Creon's wish for a completely secular world. This "sign" is the first phenomenon that occurs after Creon's burial of Polynices. One might expect a sign sent by the gods, some prodigy to mark the gods' approval, but the gods remain silent; here there is only the cry of a human voice.

In the final scene of the play it may appear that Sophocles asserts the power of the gods and the futility of human effort, but we think of Creon, not the gods, as we witness his recognition of his love for his son and his own vulnerability. Creon discovers that his own rule and power are bound up with the necessity of acknowledging kin and community, the necessity that Antigone heeds. The man who had asserted his absolute authority and autonomy now returns to Thebes, bearing his son's body and having seen the complete collapse of the family and social structure by which he defined that authority. Without family and city, as he says, he is "nothing more than nothing" (1325).

Creon's despair at the end of *Antigone* strikes few critics as either ennobling or convincing, as he seems to lack the "talent for suffering."[40] Indeed, Creon had dissociated himself from human suffering earlier in the play when he professed himself untouched by those personal interests that subvert the state; instead, he was the one who inflicted pain on others. Accordingly, his headlong descent into suffering at the play's end functions as dramatic retribution for his ignorance of the agony of death and loss. It is in this sense, once again, that his story parallels and yet differs from that of Hector. Hector's prophetic insight in the moment of dying is his own, not granted by the gods; Homer thus presents Hector's end as not different from his life, in which he upheld the value of secular wisdom and experience. Creon, too, presents himself explicitly in the be-

---

40. Waldock, p. 125. Reinhardt concludes that Creon is "piled around with misfortune rather than struck at in the root of his being" (92).

ginning of the play as committed to human rather than divine concerns, even as we can see that he wishes to be like a god. But it is humans, not the gods, who suffer; the play thus portrays Creon's education in suffering as the essence of the purely secular life for which he himself had originally made such great claims.

It is primarily through the power of speech, against silence, that Creon's suffering is distinguished from Antigone's, as Creon becomes "nothing" in his disaster, whereas Antigone leaves the stage as herself. She has clearly lost in her battle for any kind of political autonomy, in her effort to counteract Creon's *kērygma* (the Chorus, not Antigone, makes him change his mind). Further, neither the other characters in the play nor the gods confer heroic status on her.[41] While the "punishment" of Creon may be seen as her vindication, Creon never mentions her again, nor does Tiresias defend her directly in his prophecy. Yet she leaves the stage, neither abject nor resigned to oblivion, but proclaiming her importance as the last of the Cadmeans. While Creon speaks his "sentence" of death, Antigone responds by invoking the gods and the city of Thebes, calling upon the Chorus to look on her and acknowledge her right to have buried Polynices (940–43). Antigone's last act on stage is thus an act of apostrophe or invocation, meant to establish the presence and power of her own voice.[42] For her, it matters little that neither god nor city responds; for one last time, Antigone relies on her voice to define herself, as she claims her link to her city, her lineage, and the gods of her race. Antigone is denied personal and political autonomy in the city of Thebes—what she cannot have as a woman; yet at the same time Antigone main-

41. As Knox observes, "the gods do not praise Antigone, nor does anyone else in the play—except the young man who loves her so passionately that he cannot bear to live without her." See intro. to *Antigone*, in *Sophocles: The Three Theban Plays*, trans. Robert Fagles, intro. and notes by Bernard Knox (New York: Viking, 1982), p. 37.

42. See Jonathan Culler, "Apostrophe," *Diacritics* 7 (1977): 59–69, esp. p. 62.

tains her freedom of speech in public, which was the essence of freedom in Athens, where the worst punishment of exile was considered the loss of *parrēsia* or "free speech."[43] Antigone speaks, too, as the bride of death, both in this world and beyond; like Hector, she has the authority that those on the brink of death possess over the living, and yet she already stands apart from the rest of the citizens, who must find a way to rule in the days to come.

Creon's loss of his power to invoke and command marks the loss of his role in the family and the city. Creon, too, laments his disaster, but his speech lacks the ceremony and self-reflection of Antigone's. Crying forth the ritual sound of wailing, *aiai*, he calls himself wretched (*deilaios*) (1306–11). Creon's penultimate gesture, matching Antigone's, is to utter a prayer for death. It may be addressed to the gods, but it is heard only by the Chorus, who refuse to answer the prayer: "That will come," they say, "but now we must do what is before us" (1323–24). When Creon protests that he prayed for what he desires most, the Chorus answers that he must not pray now (1337). Creon thus ends in the world he created for himself, where "fate" is inflexible, yet there are no gods to hear his prayers. The gods will not help Creon, and he can no longer help himself. His words become meaningless when he himself becomes "nothing," having lost his family and his city. Earlier, Haemon compared Creon to writing tablets which, when unfolded, are blank.[44] In the end, Creon fulfills that image, becoming someone who is nothing, a voice which is *asēmos*, "without significance."

In the *Iliad*, Hector's defiance of prophecy plays out a conflict of discourse in the struggle between man and god for the right to declare *anankē*. In *Antigone*, Sophocles dramatizes that conflict in the context of the city, where the king strives to emulate the gods in making the signs of "fate," and king, prophet, and citizen compete for the right to speak for the city's needs and future. Antigone loses this battle when Creon condemns her to death, just as Hector must die, according to the sentence of "fate." But Creon is silenced by the gods—and by the playwright. Both Creon and Antigone threaten the order of the city and are destroyed, but Sophocles gives the victory to her, in the dramatic authority of her voice. Although the gods themselves never answer her pleas for recognition, her voice commands the audience's and Chorus' attention. Creon, however, trails off in inarticulate confusion, just as he has no recognizable "self" when stripped of his roles of *tyrannos*, husband, and father. Antigone never loses her ability to speak for herself, and in this way, is given her freedom. Thus it is she, not Creon, who is Hector's heir, and she who most closely imitates his defiance of fatal authority. But Antigone is not only Hector's heir; she is also the forerunner of her own father, Oedipus, who in *Oedipus the King* masters human speech in his pride and his shame.

CHAPTER 4

Speech and Silence:
Oedipus the King

The response to prophecy informs all of *Oedipus the King*, beginning with Oedipus's consulting the Oracle to save the city and ending with Creon's sending once again to Delphi for Apollo's sanction. In *Antigone*, Creon's response to prophecy only enhances his portrayal as a tyrant. But Oedipus's entire life is an answer to oracular prediction. As in *Antigone*, the context is political; Oedipus, however, combines the defiance of Antigone and the tyranny of Creon, for even as Oedipus resists the tyrannical silence of the gods, he threatens to destroy the city in his effort to speak his own story.

Like the Sphinx's riddle, which brings together the ages of man, *Oedipus the King* merges Oedipus's many encounters with Apollo and his prophet, which are all encounters with silence. In each incident—his first consultation of the Oracle about his parents' identity, his sending to Delphi about the city's plague, and his conflict with Apollo's servant, Tiresias— Oedipus cannot make god and prophet answer fully. When he asks the Oracle and later Tiresias who his parents are, they tell him only of his future—that he will kill his father and marry his mother, or discover those crimes. When he asks Apollo, through Creon, how he can save the city from the plague,

Apollo gives only half an answer: expel the murderer, says Apollo, but he leaves it for Oedipus to name the criminal.

Plutarch wrote in his *Moralia* that we learn silence from the gods, speech from man.[1] So in *Oedipus the King* silence is associated with the gods and their mysteries and speech with Oedipus. In Chapter 1, I described the language of the gods as ironic and ambiguous, and thus full of silences. In *Oedipus the King*, when the Oracle speaks, it is only to mask its silence about the truth, which Oedipus must learn. In *Antigone* it is a sign of Creon's desire for godlike tyranny that he would silence others; but *Oedipus the King* marks Oedipus's confrontation with gods by their silences. His original encounter as a young man with the horror of Delphic silence is reflected in his later resistance to any form of silence, but especially the silence of Tiresias, the prophet who imitates Apollo.

Like Antigone, Oedipus is characterized throughout the play as a person who believes in speaking freely. When this play's politically taciturn Creon hesitates to report the Oracle's mandate in front of the citizens, Oedipus insists that he speak publicly (*es pantas auda*, 93). Even in his shame at the end, Oedipus wants to tell the Chorus of his pain, while Creon wishes to shut him away in the house. But he is not content merely to speak himself; he also forces others to speak.[2] His speech is at once, in Benjamin's words, the "free spontaneous utterance of the creature" and a defense against entrapment in the gods' silence; it is through his speech that he tries to control his life and the events in the world around him.

Oedipus's first encounter with "audible" silence in Sophocles' play comes when he asks the Chorus to tell him what they know of Laius's murderer. The text implies two silences: the first after he asks that they reveal the murderer, even if he is one of them (226), and the second after he asks them to tell

---

1. *Moralia* 505f.

2. See Charles Segal, *Tragedy and Civilization: An Interpretation of Sophocles* (Cambridge: Harvard University Press, 1981), p. 244

whether the criminal is an alien (232). These two moments of silence replicate Apollo's partial silence, implicit in the oracle's omission of the murderer's name, and they provoke Oedipus to call a curse of silence down on the unknown silent criminal. If the citizens are silent, he says (*ei d'au siōpēsesthe*, 233), protecting either themselves or others, he will order all of them to shun the criminal, "neither receive him nor speak to him" (238). Not only does Oedipus's speech thus evoke (as do all his other speeches) the monstrous silence of the unspoken truth, but Oedipus also calls the curse of silence down upon himself.

Oedipus's struggle with the silence of his people, the prophet, and the gods, which becomes his defiance of prophecy, takes its shape both from the epic tradition and from the Delphic Oracle's political and religious role in Athenian society. On one level, his actions replay the defiance of Hector. On another level, Oedipus's political actions with regard to the Oracle have a double reference. First, his behavior echoes that of Athenian politicians, who knew how to manipulate oracular signs to promote their own policies for Athens' defense. Second, his abuse of the prophet Tiresias, resembling the behavior of Creon in *Antigone*, identifies him as a *tyrannos*.

Herodotus and Plutarch, believers in prophecy of quite different eras, both relate a well-known incident in Athenian history in which the politician Themistocles is said to have made divine signs fit his own purposes. Herodotus writes that when the Persians threatened Athens, the Athenians consulted the Delphic Oracle and were directed to flee the city since all was lost.[3] Rather than accept this advice, they again went to the

---

3. Herodotus 7.141–43. There is some question of the authenticity of this story; what is important for our purposes is that Herodotus seems to have regarded such behavior as patriotic rather than reprehensible. See Joseph Fontenrose, *The Delphic Oracle: Its Responses and Operations with a Catalogue of Responses* (Berkeley: University of California Press, 1978), pp. 124–28, and Roland Crahay, *La Littérature oraculaire chez Hérodote* (Paris: Belles Lettres, 1956), pp. 294–304, on the authenticity of this oracle. Fontenrose states, "So we must conclude that these two responses are dubious at best;

Oracle, asking the god "to give some better oracle concerning our country." The Oracle answered once again with the famous oracle of the wooden walls: "Zeus grants this to Athena, that the wooden wall alone shall be unravaged, for the profit of you and your children" (7.141.6–7). It counseled that they should not wait for the coming of the army, but turn their backs, until the day of battle comes: "Holy Salamis, you shall destroy the children of women, when men sow, or when they harvest" (11–12). The new answer elicited many different interpretations, as Herodotus tells us. Did the Oracle mean the wooden wall of the citadel, or, metaphorically, the "wall" of the fleet? If so, the people wondered what the reference to Salamis signified. Did it not suggest a defeat at the island of Salamis? As Herodotus reports, it was Themistocles, long an advocate of the Athenian fleet, who delivered the city from its quandary: "This man said that the interpreters [*tous chrēs-mologous*] had not quite accurately hit on the meaning" (7.143.5–6). Themistocles insisted that if the Oracle meant to predict a defeat at Salamis, it would have used the phrase "wretched Salamis" (*ō schetliē Salamis*) instead of "holy Salamis" (*ō theiē Salamis*), and so he advised them to prepare to fight on their ships, as these were the "wooden walls" in which they had been told to trust. The Athenians found Themistocles' reading preferable to the reading of the interpreters (143.3–5). Themistocles was, of course, proved "right," insofar as the Athenians succeeded brilliantly by relying on the fleet, but it was he who *made* it true through his advocacy of the Athenian navy.

Plutarch, much later, makes explicit what Herodotus only implies, that Themistocles in fact seized control of the Oracle's authority to suit his plan to evacuate the city and rely on the fleet for defense.[4] Plutarch prefaces his account of the same

---

if authentic they are extraordinary and unusual pronouncements of the Delphic Oracle" (p. 128).

4. See Martin P. Nilsson, *Cults, Myths, Oracles, and Politics in Ancient Greece* (Lund: Gleerup, 1951), p. 124.

scene with a description of Themistocles' response to the Persian advance. He tells how "then indeed, Themistocles, failing to influence the majority with human reasoning, provided divine signs and oracles for them, just as if he were erecting a machine in a tragedy [*hōsper en tragōidia(i) mēchanēn aras*]; he took as a sign the serpent which seemed to have disappeared then from the sacred precinct; and when the priests found that the daily sacrifices to the serpent were untouched, they announced to the multitude—Themistocles putting the words in their mouth [*tou Themistokleous logon didontos*]—that the goddess had left the city behind and was leading them to the sea."[5] After that, Plutarch says, he also tried to convince the people with his reading of the oracle of the wooden wall, until finally he got his way. Plutarch thus associates Themistocles' interpretation of the oracle with his invention of the serpent prodigy, in which he "gave the word" to the priests, clothing his own ideas and thoughts in sacred authority when other means failed. Further, both sign and oracle are compared to a tragic *mēchanē*, which can mean contrivance or, more specifically, the machine in which the gods were brought down to the stage. In either case it suggests the application of a "supernatural"—and artificial—solution to a human problem.

It is difficult, of course, to draw any close parallels between Oedipus and Themistocles, or to claim that Sophocles counted on his audience to remember the politician, who died thirty years before *Oedipus the King* was performed.[6] Yet the incident suggests how prophecy might have been understood and used for the city's sake in fifth-century Athens. Themistocles, as a politician, made the gods and prophets speak the words he thought necessary to save his city. In *Oedipus the King*, Oedi-

5. Plutarch, *Life of Themistocles*, 10.1. Text from *Plutarch's Lives*, vol. 2 (Cambridge: Harvard University Press, 1948).

6. Bernard Knox suggests in *Oedipus at Thebes* that Oedipus himself resembles Themistocles, as the intelligent amateur, "the Thucydidean archetype of the Athenian democratic character at its best" (New Haven: Yale University Press, 1957; rpt. New York: Norton, 1971), p. 73.

pus begins by taking up Apollo's oracle as a means to save the city, and then reinforces it with his own curse. Oedipus goes a step further than Themistocles, however; when Tiresias's refusal to name the murderer seems to threaten the civic order, as Oedipus sees it, and prophecy seems inadequate, Oedipus pronounces his *phatis*, his story that Creon and Tiresias conspired to kill Laius, an accusation that reduces Tiresias's words to the manifestation of a political conspiracy. Unlike Themistocles, Oedipus does not simply present his ideas as a divine mandate, contradicting the *chrēsmologoi*. Oedipus competes with the Oracle and Tiresias, setting himself up as the city's only "prophet" by attempting to find explanations for events in human stories and testimony. What happens, of course, is that his efforts lead him eventually to confirm Apollo's and Tiresias's words. It appears that in this play Sophocles is not willing to allow the human word full power to govern the world.

The play's title, *Oedipus Tyrannos*, draws attention to Oedipus's political role in the city, which is inextricably linked to his effort to present himself as a new "prophet" for the city. Most scholars who have contrasted Oedipus and *Antigone*'s Creon find, as Webster puts it, that "Oedipus is the good ruler in spite of his defects, and Creon the bad ruler in spite of his virtues."[7] A comparison of their opening speeches suggests some of the initial differences. In his speech, Creon emphasizes that the citizens must put the state's interests before their own; Oedipus, however, proclaims his own obligation to the citizens, his private pain for the public cause, declaring that while each of them feels only his own pain, "my spirit mourns for the city, for you, and for myself" (63–64). Both Creon and Oedipus each identify their private will with the public opinion. Creon,

7. T. B. L. Webster, *An Introduction to Sophocles* (Oxford: Clarendon, 1936), p. 63. See also Victor Ehrenberg, *Sophocles and Pericles* (Oxford: Blackwell, 1954), and Thomas Gould, "The Innocence of Oedipus: The Philosophers on *Oedipus the King*," *Arion* 4 (1965): 582–611, esp p. 599; and Knox, pp. 53–61.

however, seems to force his will on the city, whereas Oedipus makes the public will his private desire.[8]

The frequent repetition of the word *tyrannos* in the play raises the question whether Oedipus is indeed a "tyrant." In some cases in Greek tragedy the word *tyrannos* is interchangable with the word *basileus*, "king"; at other places, *tyrannos* means more what we understand by "tyrant," a ruler who has wrongfully seized power and who rules unjustly.[9] While for many scholars Oedipus does not really resemble the Greek tyrant described by Plato in the *Republic*,[10] some see him on the "verge of tyranny"[11] in his irrational anger, his apparently illegitimate assumption of power (which turns out to be legitimate), and his commission of the "paradigmatic" tyrannical crimes of incest and parricide.[12] Plato and others attribute to the tyrant the transgression of the boundaries that separate human from beast.[13] To them, the tyrant is a monster, a wolf, an animal masked as a human being.[14]

More significant for this study, however, Oedipus has also been suspected of wanting to be a god in Thebes. In the *parodos*, the Chorus come to Oedipus as suppliants, as if to a god,[15] although the priest denies that they equate him with the gods

---

8. See Seth Benardete, "Sophocles' *Oedipus Tyrannos*," in *Sophocles: A Collection of Critical Essays*, ed. Thomas Woodard (Englewood Cliffs, N.J.: Prentice-Hall, 1966), pp. 105–21, on the private and public in relation to Oedipus.

9. On the meaning of *tyrannos* as simply "king" or "tyrant," see Ehrenberg, pp. 66–67; Gould, p. 599; Knox, pp. 53–61.

10. Knox, p. 59. See also Diego Lanza, *Il tiranno e il suo pubblico* (Torino: Einaudi, 1977), pp. 140–48.

11. Ehrenberg, p.67.

12. Benardete, p. 108. See also Vincent Farenga, "The Paradigmatic Tyrant: Greek Tyranny and the Ideology of the Proper," *Helios* 8 (1981): 1–31.

13. See Farenga, p. 2.

14. See Plato, *Republic* 8.566.

15. Ehrenberg, p. 67: "The suppliant people approach him almost as a god (2.31f.), and he is honoured as a saviour, as *Soter* (46f.)"; see also Knox, pp. 59–60, and Cedric H. Whitman, *Sophocles: A Study of Heroic Humanism* (Cambridge: Harvard University Press, 1951), p. 125.

(31). Later, when the Chorus has prayed to the Olympians, Oedipus responds, "You pray [*aiteis*]. If you want what you pray for—if, hearing my words, you accept them and turn back the plague, you will gain strength and relief from evil" (216–17), words which echo the style of the Delphic Oracle.[16] But if he thus seems to embrace a god's role, it is not as Creon did, by imitating the impersonal and severe qualities of the divine voice, but rather by mimicking the god and Oracle in his role as granter of prayers, *sōtēr* or "savior." Oedipus is a "humanized" god, responsive and benevolent, the city's guardian, more father than fate. Further, in contrast to *Antigone*'s Creon, Oedipus, until he argues with Tiresias, seems remarkably pious.[17] When Apollo delivers his mandate to expel the curse on the land, Oedipus takes this as his responsibility, for the sake of Apollo, his city, and himself, proclaiming that "rightly you see me as an ally [*symmachon*], honoring both the land and the god" (135–36). He transforms Apollo's oracle into his own curse on the murderer and those who protect him, identifying his own will and words with the god's.

Oedipus's character as *tyrannos* thus seems different from Creon's. Oedipus is both better and worse than Creon, worse in his crimes that are eventually revealed, but from his first appearance better as a benevolent and god-fearing, if authoritative, leader. He is not seen to pose a threat to the city until the entrance of the prophet Tiresias. Oedipus intends, by sending for Tiresias, to receive further divine assistance in his task. When Tiresias refuses to cooperate, however, Oedipus treats Tiresias's silence as a betrayal of Thebes (330–31). In *Antigone*, Creon's rejection of Tiresias climaxes his rivalry with the gods. In *Oedipus the King*, Tiresias's arrival initiates the conflict between Apollo's signs and Oedipus's voice—a conflict that

16. Knox comments that Oedipus's words "accept and promise fulfillment of the choral prayer . . . and are phrased in what is a typical formula of the Delphic oracle" (p. 160).

17. See Ehrenberg, p. 67: "He is also a pious man who believes in oracles, respects the bonds of family, fears and hates impurity."

strikes at the roots of the city's order, which is based on the cooperation between sacred and secular interests.

The Tiresias whom Oedipus encounters is a far more complex figure than *Antigone*'s Tiresias. Sophocles did not strongly characterize the earlier Tiresias, but presented him solely as the gods' representative in Creon's secular world. In *Oedipus the King*, however, Tiresias's character makes him, in Reinhardt's words, a "walking enigma," half "superhuman, half only too human."[18] In a sense Tiresias is Oedipus's double, as Oedipus, too, represents an enigma in the duality of his being.[19] Yet Oedipus and Tiresias are also opposites, the mortal facing the riddling god. Tiresias directly mimics the Oracle, which, in Heraclitus's well-known formula, "does not speak or hide but signifies [*sēmainei*]."[20] On stage, Tiresias *is* the Oracle, the divine mind in human flesh, a figure of divinity expressed in human speech. Like the Oracle, too, he seems to respond to supplication and yet finally refuses to respond, angering the king.

Tiresias's most vital secret is the secret of Oedipus's past, his parentage, and his crimes. Although later he will tell Oedipus of his future—his discovery, blindness, and exile—the scene focuses on Tiresias's ability to tell the "true" story of Laius's murder. But Tiresias does not tell his story until Oedipus, angered by Tiresias's silence, produces his own solution to the mystery: "Know that I think that you conspired to do the deed—and did it, except for killing him with your hands; if you could see, I would say that you did the deed alone" (348–49). Tiresias's response is swift and brutal: "Is that true [*alēthes*?]? Then I bid you to abide by the decree [*kērygmati*] that

18. Karl Reinhardt, *Sophocles*, trans. H. Harvey and D. Harvey (1947; rpt. New York: Barnes & Noble, 1979), p. 104.

19. Jean-Pierre Vernant and Pierre Vidal-Naquet, *Tragedy and Myth in Ancient Greece*, trans. Janet Lloyd (Atlantic Highlands, N.J.: Humanities Press, 1981), p. 90

20. Frag. 93, in H. Diels, *Die Fragmente der Vorsokratiker*, 7th ed. (Berlin: Weidmann, 1954). See Reinhardt, p. 104; Benardete, p. 113.

you yourself pronounced, from this day on to speak neither to me nor to these people, for you are the unholy polluter of the land" (350–53). Tiresias insists that the truth is strong in *him* (356). Oedipus, however, has already set up the terms of the *agon* as a contest of contradictory stories about the murder.

While Oedipus, like *Antigone*'s Creon, accuses Tiresias of being just another greedy fortune-teller (388–89), his attack against the prophet's authority goes far beyond this accusation, as he attempts to strip him and his words of divinity. Oedipus creates a situation in which Tiresias's words seem to have no value, when, as René Girard says, he makes Tiresias's accusation seem "simply an act of reprisal arising from the hostile exchange of a tragic debate."[21] Tiresias seems to admit this, in effect, when Oedipus asks who taught him this "word" or story (*rhēma*), for he cannot believe it was derived through his *technē*, "mantic craft" (357). Tiresias answers that he "learned" it from Oedipus: "From you—you forced me to speak unwillingly" (358); Oedipus, not divine inspiration, motivated Tiresias's speech.

Oedipus taunts Tiresias further, saying that he has neither the right nor the power to speak the truth. For him, Tiresias's physical infirmity indicates mental incapacity. When Oedipus asks whether Tiresias thinks he can keep on talking this way (368), and Tiresias answers yes, for there is strength in the truth (369), Oedipus retaliates, "Indeed there is, but not in you; in you there is no truth, for you are blind in your ears and your mind as well as your eyes" (370–71).

Oedipus reminds Tiresias that it was he, Oedipus, not the prophet, who was able to solve the riddle of the Sphinx (cf. 390–98). Just as Oedipus claims that his tale of Creon's and Tiresias's conspiracy supplants any Tiresias can tell, so he demonstrates that he, with his own mind, can supplant the prophet

21. René Girard, *Violence and the Sacred*, trans. Patrick Gregory (Baltimore: Johns Hopkins University Press, 1977), pp. 70–71.

in Thebes: "I came, Oedipus who knows nothing, I stopped [the Sphinx], I succeeded, by my intelligence, without learning anything from birds [*out'ap'oiōnōn...mathōn*]" (397–98). Like Themistocles, Oedipus has taken over when the prophet and gods seem to have failed the city, acting himself both as an interpreter and a provider of answers. Tiresias becomes, from Oedipus's perspective, merely a political antagonist, a schemer in a conspiracy to overthrow the rightful ruler of Thebes.

Thus Oedipus attacks the prophet with a twofold strategy: he attempts to go him one better as a revealer of past secrets and a solver of riddles, and he places the prophet in an essentially political and secular setting, stripping him of sacred privilege. Like Hector, Oedipus is at least temporarily successful in outwitting and debasing the prophet. C. M. Bowra may call Oedipus's tale of conspiracy a "hallucination,"[22] but it has enough reality *in the play* to render Tiresias's words ineffective, insofar as neither Oedipus nor the Chorus believes them. As Oedipus says, Tiresias speaks in vain (*hōs matēn eirēsetai*, 365), when Oedipus does not even seem to hear him, and the Chorus will not convict their king merely on the basis of Tiresias's words. The Chorus, while they respect the wisdom of Zeus and Apollo, question whether "the *mantis*, among men, should be right more than myself, for there is no certain means of judging the truth; but one man may excel another in skill [*sophian*]" (499–503). It is not simply that Tiresias has no proof;[23] Oedipus has made it seem that he and Tiresias are merely rivals, competing in their skill, speaking the same language. In these terms, this is not an oracular consultation, in Oedipus's view, but a citizens' court of law, where men are

---

22. C. M. Bowra, *Sophoclean Tragedy* (Oxford: Clarendon, 1944), p. 195.
23. As Whitman says, "Tiresias offered no proof for what he said, but based it simply on his prophetic art, which is not sufficient in this case to convince even the naive Chorus" (p. 131).

equal, and the victory will go to the man who speaks better in his own defense.[24]

If Oedipus means to supplant the sacred with the secular,[25] he succeeds, for the moment, with respect to the past. What Oedipus cannot grasp, as Hector cannot, is the riddle of the future. Toward the end of the episode, Tiresias tells Oedipus of his future (412–28), but Oedipus says he hears only absurdities (*mōra*, 433). Tiresias taunts Oedipus, too, with the one secret of the past Oedipus feels he does not know for sure: "I brought forth these things, which you think are absurd," he says, "but your parents, who brought you forth, found them wise" (435–36). Startled, Oedipus asks him who his parents are, but Tiresias only says, "This day shall give you life and destroy you" (438). As the Oracle did, Tiresias answers Oedipus's question about the past with an enigmatic prediction of the future. Tiresias's prophecy thus suggests a radical difference between Oedipus's and Tiresias's language and knowledge, however alike the two men may seem in this scene. While both Oedipus and Tiresias are riddlers, because their language is fraught with double meaning, Tiresias's ambiguity is informed, whereas Oedipus only thinks he speaks without silences, hidden meanings, or ambiguity. The audience, of course, has a double view of the play. They see Oedipus's viewpoint, entirely in the present tense and in a purely secular world, as well as Tiresias's, a view from the future into the present and past.

The stalemate created in this scene, and in the scene with Creon which follows, ends with the entrance of Jocasta, who talks Oedipus into permitting Creon to go unpunished. When Oedipus then complains that Tiresias blames him for Laius's murder, Jocasta argues that no human has true prophetic skill (*broteion ouden mantikēs echon technēs*, 709). She offers to show him *sēmeia* or signs (710) as proof of this contention.

---

24. Knox, in his analysis of this scene, notes that it resembles a legal trial (p. 86).

25. Benardete, p. 114.

Jocasta's *sēmeia*, like Oedipus's accusations, amount to a kind of anti-oracle. She opposes what she believes to be the real story (*phatis*, 716) of Laius's death against the Oracle's *chrēsmos*. So she tells how "an oracle [*chrēsmos*] came to Laius once, I would not say from Apollo himself, but from those under him" (711–12), which said that he should be killed by his own son. "But, as the report [*phatis*] goes" (715), Laius was killed by strangers at the place where three roads meet. In this story, Jocasta in effect repeats Oedipus's strategy against Tiresias. First, she represents the oracle to Laius as human discourse, not the direct words of Apollo but the stories of priests. She thus renders the oracle fallible, just as Oedipus emphasizes Tiresias's human failings to leave him open to doubt. Second, Jocasta, like Oedipus, sets the human word against the mantic sign, her *phatis* against the *chrēsmos*. It is a further irony that the word *phatis* can mean "oracle" or "prophecy," as well as "report" or "rumor."[26] Jocasta has found her own "oracle" in human testimony.

Jocasta's attack against prophecy has a different result than Oedipus's attack: her *phatis* contains a phrase, "the place where three roads meet" (716), which catches Oedipus's attention. Oedipus sees suddenly that he indeed might be Laius's murderer, having killed a man at such a place. Afraid that "the prophet can see after all" (747), he calls for the herdsman, the only surviving witness, to retell his story, and he narrates for Jocasta his flight from Corinth, the murder at the crossroads, and his triumphant arrival in Thebes. Rather than turning to the god, Oedipus again relies on human testimony to establish his guilt or innocence. When Jocasta wants to know why Oedipus is so eager to see the herdsman, Oedipus responds, "If his words match yours, I shall escape suffering" (839–40). Jocasta had said that the herdsman spoke of robbers who killed Laius, not just one man (842), and if the herdsman holds to the same number (844–45), Oedipus is innocent. Oedipus thus focuses

26. Segal, p. 237.

not on the correspondence of his experience with the prophet's words but rather on matching his experience to the herdsman's story. In his search for the murderer, the question of prophecy's truth seems secondary.

Jocasta and Oedipus give the herdsman's story an authority that supplants that of prophecy. To reassure Oedipus, Jocasta insists that the herdsman "cannot retract [his story] now" (*kouk estin autō[i] touto g'ekbalein palin*, 849), having once told his story as she retold it. She attributes to his words the immutability of the prophetic word, echoing what Tiresias says in *Antigone* when he boasts that his words, once spoken, can be neither called back nor avoided. The herdsman himself is the only person other than Tiresias who knows the secret of Oedipus's birth and crimes. When confronted by Oedipus, he acts as Tiresias did—he, too, would rather not say what he knows and pretends to have forgotten (1141). But the herdsman is also different from Tiresias in that words are not enough to make him speak. By twisting back his arms, Oedipus makes him suffer pain, which he does not inflict on Tiresias and cannot inflict on Apollo. It is this last step, the infliction of pain to break silence, which forces Oedipus's own initiation into inexpressible pain.

Indeed, it is the herdsman's *phatis* that brings Oedipus to realize that Apollo's oracle has been fulfilled. Oedipus and Jocasta contend that simple facts and human testimony contradict and thus invalidate the oracles from Delphi. When Oedipus confesses his earlier visit to the Oracle, Jocasta relies on an apparent fact—the destruction of the infant Oedipus—to invalidate the Oracle's predictions. The Messenger's report that Polybus is dead, too, seems certain proof that all oracles and signs mean nothing, as Oedipus exults: "Why then," he asks, "look to the hearth of the Pythia, or the birds that cry above, who prophesied that I would kill my father?" (964–68). In his rejection of the oracle, Oedipus depends on the Messenger's accuracy, an expectation the Messenger lives up to only too well, for he knows Polybus is not truly Oedipus's father. When

Jocasta finally realizes that Oedipus is her son, she attempts to discredit the Messenger, just as she had earlier devalued prophecy, calling the Messenger's words just vain speech, empty talk (*ta de rhēthenta boulou mēde memnēsthai matēn*, 1057). But Oedipus pushes through to the end, as the herdsman's report intersects with the oracle, and the story that Oedipus believed would contradict Apollo's oracle becomes identical to it.

As the play approaches this *peripeteia*, Oedipus's attempt to create a secular order through human stories seems less and less an affirmation of the city's concerns and more a tyrannical attack on order. At the play's beginning, when he is faced with a world that seems confused and inexplicable, Oedipus tries to control the city's crisis by finding the words for it, first in his invention of Creon's and Tiresias's conspiracy, and when that strategy fails, through his attempts to reconstruct the past. But as that effort becomes more and more personal, a question of *Oedipus*'s past, Oedipus seems to threaten directly the stability that the fulfillment of oracles represents, without establishing any new structure. After Jocasta first declares that prophecy has no meaning, the Chorus sings of its fear that Apollo's oracles will not be fulfilled, even though their fulfillment means disaster for Oedipus: "Never again will I go, reverent, to the sacred navel of the land, nor to the temple at Abae, or Olympus, if these oracles are not fulfilled for all mortals to point at" (898–903). "Why should I dance?" the Chorus asks (896): If oracles are not fulfilled, there is no divine prescience, or even presence on earth, and Oedipus's own words and presence do not seem a sufficient substitute.

Oedipus himself, nearing the moment of recognition, thinks less of the city's misery than of the mystery of his own identity, as he is willing to sacrifice civic order, or at least those fictions that maintain civic order, to gain complete autonomy and self-knowledge. Trying to encourage Oedipus, Jocasta asks, "Why do men fear, when chance rules, and there is no clear foresight [*pronoia*] of anything?" (977–78). So Oedipus, on the verge of knowing his birth, proclaims that "I count myself the son of Chance" (1080), who is the goddess who personifies lack of cosmic order.[27] It is at this moment that Oedipus comes closest to tyranny, insofar as his will diverges furthest from the city's interests. The moment demands Oedipus's rapid recognition of the oracle's fulfillment for the city's sake, as the vindication of the gods' words and their order at whatever cost. Here the playwright seems ultimately on the side of the gods, who, as Benardete says, "want the authority of all the oracles, i.e., their own authority, maintained even at the expense of human morality."[28] Oedipus loses in his attempt to govern his city and himself through his own speech, when fighting against the power of religious and civic fictions of order.

Taking Oedipus's recognition of the oracle's truth as the "lesson" of the play, some scholars describe the last episode as a portrayal of a humbler yet wiser Oedipus, broken by the gods.[29] Others see Oedipus reasserting his authority and intelligence even in his suffering.[30]

Oedipus's own words about his relationship with Apollo are quite complex. When the Chorus asks him which of the *daimones* drove him to blind himself (1328), Oedipus answers that it was both Apollo and himself: "He brought to pass these evils and my sufferings, but I, in my misery, struck my eyes with my own hands" (1330–32). This intersection between the god's words and Oedipus's actions and words also appears in Oedipus' demand that Creon fulfill the Oracle's mandate to expel the murderer, thereby also fulfilling his own curse. When Creon hesitates to decide Oedipus's fate, Oedipus reminds him that the Oracle has already spoken, asking for the murderer's death or banishment: "The voice [*phatis*] of the god was clear to all—to destroy the parricide, myself, unholy" (1440–41). But as Oedipus calls on Apollo's authority, he acknowledges

27. Knox, p. 166.
28. Benardete, p. 113.
29. See Bowra, p. 210, and Gould, e.g.
30. See Whitman, p. 142; Knox, chap. 5.

that he, too, has commanded, as he says to the Chorus: "I deprived myself, myself commanding that all should shun the blasphemer" (1381–82). Oedipus thus apparently sees in his disaster not simply the tyranny of the god's word over his own life but a consonance between his commands and the god's pronouncements, even as human stories came to correspond with the Oracle's version of Oedipus' past. At the same time, he certainly tries to gain control of his own future, giving orders to Creon for the burial of his wife and for his children's future.[31] But Oedipus clearly pushes Creon, the city's new leader, too far. When Oedipus begs that his daughters not be taken away, Creon reminds Oedipus that he must no longer wish to rule in all things (*panta mē boulou kratein*, 1522). Like Creon at the end of *Antigone*, Oedipus no longer has *kratos* ("authority"), and his voice has lost the power to command in the city and direct its future.

Yet while Oedipus has lost his power to command, he has not lost his voice. Oedipus does not slip into the life of silence he has cursed upon himself and which indeed he seems at first to seek, when he asks that Creon drive him out of the country "to where no one will ever speak to me" (1437). As at the play's beginning, in the end Oedipus finds silence unbearable; he must speak his pain, even though his crimes are unspeakable and his pain impossible to articulate. When Oedipus first appears before the Chorus after the catastrophe, he does indeed seem broken, unconscious of his own voice in his pain. He cries out to the Chorus, "Where is my voice [*phthogga*] flying, so violently?" (1310). His very voice seems "disembodied,"[32] not his own, in the initial moments of his pain. Yet, even as he asks these questions, he responds to the Chorus as the sound of another human voice: "I recognize your voice, clearly, even in this darkness" (1326–27). The final episode suggests that

---

31. See Knox, p. 189.
32. Segal, p. 242.

for Oedipus, the human voice, with human touch, is more than ever the identifying mark of human nature, the mark of the presence of others and of himself.

For Oedipus, stripped of his position in the city, blind and helpless, his last resource of power is his voice.[33] Although he loses the power of the political command, he never loses the authority of self-naming, as Creon does in *Antigone*. Creon calls himself "nothing more than nothing"; Oedipus, however, proclaims his name to the Chorus in all his shame: "This," he says, "is the lot of Oedipus [*tout'elach' Oidipous*]," (1366). In contrast to Creon, whose authority is defined solely by his political and familial position in *Antigone*, Sophocles' Oedipus is meant to have authority by "nature," which is revealed even in the experience of his suffering, when he alone has the right to speak of what it is to be Oedipus.

Can it be said, then, that in this play Oedipus ends, as Hector does, by discovering his own prophetic voice? He has come, certainly, to know the past as Tiresias does and to understand his present identity and condition, but does Sophocles bestow on him a vision or right to speak of the future? Charles Segal concludes that Oedipus is at the end "a second Tiresias," with an "inner sight of blindness," a vision like Hector's, coming "not as a gift of the gods but as the hard acquisition of his human experience and suffering."[34] Oedipus does seem to anticipate his own future as he says to Creon: "This I know, that neither disease nor any other ill shall destroy me; I would not now have been saved from death if it were not for some terrible evil" (1455–57). But while he anticipates the future, he does not have a clear knowledge of future events, such as Hector obtains in his death. At the play's end, he has a sense of himself as a man with a future, but he does not yet have the right to know or determine it.

In this play, as in *Antigone*, Sophocles dramatizes a crisis in

33. Reinhardt, p. 130.
34. Segal, p. 246.

which humans try, and fail, to write their own stories. Oedipus's attempt to have his "plots" win out over those of the prophet and the Oracle—and the playwright—fails, because the play makes the fulfillment of prophecy a necessity for the city's survival. Sophocles suggests, in the moment when the Chorus hesitates between Tiresias's and Oedipus's versions of the past, that it might have been otherwise. Indeed, some critics see that Oedipus makes himself a scapegoat, accepting the others' story of the murder without sufficient proof and giving in to "oracular idolatry."[35] Even as Sophocles allows for the myth and the oracle to be criticized, he grants the oracle the power of truth through the agency of Oedipus himself. The playwright respects the social order such fulfillment represents, at whatever cost for the individual. Yet *Oedipus the King* also celebrates the power of human speech to represent a self, even in such a defeat. The tension between the two impulses is evident, and the only solution is to move Oedipus out of the city.

For Oedipus, as for Antigone, even in disaster the human voice achieves a dramatic or apostrophic significance without power to command. As *tyrannos*, through his abandonment of the city's cause in the search for his own identity and autonomy, Oedipus risks and loses his authority as king, and his voice is stripped of the power to rule. When Oedipus speaks at the end of the play, however, his words have little to do with politics. Sophocles moves him out of the sphere of city and gods, into the state of exile, where we find him at the beginning of *Oedipus at Colonus*, about to violate the silent grove of the Furies.

35. Sandor Goodhart, "*Leistas ephaske*: Oedipus and Laius' Many Murderers," *Diacritics* 8 (1978): 67, who follows Girard. See also Cynthia Chase, "Oedipal Textuality: Reading Freud's Reading of *Oedipus*," *Diacritics* 9 (1979): 54–68.

CHAPTER 5

The Heroic Prophet:
Oedipus at Colonus

The story of the defiance of prophecy is primarily a tale of conflict. In the Theban plays of Sophocles, men and women fight with the gods or among themselves for the right to speak the truth. The story of *Oedipus the King* remains for many people the definitive model of a man's—and king's—battle with the oracular god. Yet Sophocles did not end his account of this struggle with *Oedipus the King*. His last play, *Oedipus at Colonus*, stands as his final version of the relationship between a man's word and divine prediction. In *Antigone* and *Oedipus the King*, Sophocles represented that relationship as a conflict between Thebes' king and its prophet, Tiresias, in which both claimed the right to interpret the past and declare the future. Tiresias is absent, however, from *Oedipus at Colonus*. Instead the aged Oedipus and his daughter Ismene are the ones who bear Apollo's old and new oracles to Athens. Moreover, in this play the political situation has changed: Oedipus is no longer king, but is the object of a political conflict, as Creon and Polynices fight to have Oedipus on their side as the guarantor of blessings, while Theseus defends Oedipus's desire to stay in Colonus. An exile from his own city, Oedipus first supports Apollo's oracles and then assumes the prophet's role himself, at Athens' edge, in the sacred grove of the Eumenides. In this sense, the play is at once a sequel to *Oedipus the King*[1] and a rewriting of it, for *Oedipus at Colonus* seems "to mirror the formal design of the *Oedipus Tyrannus* and to reverse it in mirror fashion."[2] The portrayal of Oedipus's collaboration with Apollo contrasts with his defiance of Tiresias in *Oedipus the King*, just as Oedipus's scene with Tiresias in that play represents a change from Creon's scene with the prophet in the earlier *Antigone*.

Oedipus's assumption of the prophet's role would seem to violate the terms of the heroic tradition in that Oedipus becomes a collaborator with Apollo and his oracles rather than an enemy of the god and his order. Yet *Oedipus at Colonus* makes clear what is implicit in that tradition—that the hero desires to appropriate the power of the prophet's voice. We have already seen how Sophocles depicts the hero's behavior as often belying those oppositions he constructs in his defiance, as the hero begins to covet the arbitrary and unquestioned power of the gods. *Oedipus at Colonus* not only makes explicit the potential alliance and identification between human and god; it also blurs the distinction between speech and silence fundamental to the representation of power in the other plays and to the divorce between the secular and sacred which the hero creates. Oedipus's becoming a prophet in *Oedipus at Colonus* thus collapses all the oppositions that mark the conflict between hero and prophet in the earlier Theban plays.

Taking up the defiance of prophecy once again in *Oedipus*

---

1. Some scholars consider *Oedipus at Colonus* primarily a sequel to *Oedipus the King*, in which Sophocles decided to make amends to Oedipus. As Antigone puts it, here "the gods raise up the man whom they destroyed before" (394). See C. M. Bowra, *Sophoclean Tragedy* (Oxford: Clarendon, 1944), p. 308; Cedric H. Whitman, *Sophocles: A Study of Heroic Humanism* (Cambridge: Harvard University Press, 1951), p. 192.

2. Robert D. Murray, Jr., "Thought and Structure in Sophoclean Tragedy," in *Sophocles: A Collection of Critical Essays*, ed. Thomas Woodard (Englewood Cliffs, N.J.: Prentice-Hall, 1966), p. 26. See also Bernrd Seidensticker, "Beziehungen zwischen den beiden Oidipusdramen des Sophokles," *Hermes* 100 (1972): 255–74.

at Colonus, Sophocles evokes the motifs of human speech and oracular silence in a new context. In *Antigone* and *Oedipus the King* the confrontation between hero and prophet takes place in Thebes. In that city, as it is drawn by Sophocles, freedom to speak signifies that a person has both political freedom and a social identity. One of the city's worst punishments is enforced silence, in exile or isolation; it is with this punishment that Creon threatens Antigone and Oedipus threatens Laius's murderer. In the earlier plays, the speaker opposing the prophet is also the city's leader, the supposed representative of its interests and values. While he speaks for himself, he insists on his right to speak for the city as well, until it seems that he threatens to overwhelm its citizens or to abandon the city's interests entirely.

Oedipus at Colonus, however, begins and ends outside the city, in the sacred grove of the Eumenides, where a rule imposes silence.[3] When Oedipus enters the grove at the play's beginning, he sits and speaks where speaking is not allowed. Like the younger Oedipus, he is once again a violator of silence. The Chorus fear to speak near the grove and confess that they will "pass by not seeing, not speaking, moving our lips in silent prayer" (128–32). They call on Oedipus to leave the grove, to come down to where all may speak lawfully (*hina pasi nomos phōnei*, 168–69). Yet when Oedipus does consent to leave his seat, *he* is the one who refuses to speak when pressed by the Chorus to say his name. In this play Oedipus knows what is unspeakable—he later blames Creon for blasphemy in speaking of the past—and he resists the Chorus's probing.[4] This opening scene stands in sharp contrast to the central event of *Oedipus*

3. See Charles Segal, *Tragedy and Civilization: An Interpretation of Sophocles* (Cambridge: Harvard University Press, 1981), p. 392.

4. See Diskin Clay, "Unspeakable Words in Greek Tragedy," *American Journal of Philology* 103 (1982): 277–98, on the "power of the unspeakable" in Greek tragedy in the context of the Athenian law against verbal abuse and the civic context of the courts of Athens (p. 281).

the King, where it is Oedipus who forces the herdsman to reveal Oedipus's identity.

In *Oedipus at Colonus*, despite the rule of silence, the hero must speak his secret first, for his identity becomes the premise for the play's action. Thus Oedipus is at the center of a political conflict between Athens and Thebes in which his acceptance or refusal of shelter ensures military victory and political right. It has been prophesied that the city that shelters Oedipus's grave shall flourish. So Oedipus speaks to enter the realm of action, where he can act through persuasion and the speaking of blessing and curse, assent and denial.[5] Yet, when his work is done, he returns to the grove of the Eumenides once again. His grave will be a secret place and his power ensured only by Theseus's silence.

Thus at its beginning and at its end *Oedipus at Colonus* differs markedly from the first two Theban plays, both in its celebration of silence and in its merging of sacred and secular words. Antigone's and the younger Oedipus's heroism is identified with their speech, the free expression of self and identity, even as her life and his career end in disaster, while the gods maintain their silence. In this play, however, the boundary between human speech and divine silence disappears. Here human speech is given a new importance in governing human lives, as Theseus and Oedipus exchange promises for the future and Oedipus curses his sons. But Oedipus also discovers the effects of silence. In the end he enters the realm of silence which the gods had claimed as their own, just as the gods themselves break their silence to speak to Oedipus at last. In all the Theban plays, the conflict between humans is primarily verbal, in the competition of oracles, stories and proclamations that explain the past, present, and future. In *Oedipus the King*, the divine sign and human word contradict each other, as Oedipus con-

---

5. As Segal observes, "he must leave the grove, the place of silence, and return to a common ground of speech with other men" (p. 392).

trasts human testimony on Laius's murder with the prophet's and god's version of the past. In *Oedipus at Colonus*, however, Sophocles moves away from the tragic opposition of the sacred sign and secular voice. Creon and Polynices, attempting to make prophecy serve their political interests, are trapped by it when they fail. Oedipus, however, both speaks with Apollo and comes to supersede the god as the prophetic voice of the play.

In *Oedipus at Colonus*, Oedipus enters bearing an oracle pronounced by Apollo long before, which foretells Oedipus's future and the play's *telos*. When Oedipus discovers that he has wandered into the Eumenides' grove, he reveals that when Apollo first prophesied his doom, he also prophesied other things: that Oedipus should find his rest where the Eumenides reside and "be a blessing to those who have received me, and a curse to those who sent me away" (92–93). The oracle also said that he should receive *sēmeia* or "signs" to confirm these things—thunder, lightning, or earthquakes. This oracle thus marks the boundaries of the play itself, from Oedipus's entrance into the foretold grove, as the action begins, until the thunder near the end, which hails Oedipus to his secret grave. The oracle is thus a "script" for the plot, including Oedipus's acceptance in Athens and his death in Colonus, heralded by divine signs.

The Oedipus of this play eagerly accepts the oracle of Apollo as a "conventional" sign and guarantee of his future. When he discovers that he is in the Eumenides' grove, he declares that he shall never leave this place (45). When the Stranger asks him what he means by this, Oedipus replies, "This is the *synthēma* of my fortune [*symphoras*]" (46). *Synthēma* here is usually translated as "watchword," meaning a conventional sign established by prior agreement. Oedipus completes the agreement by promising to stay in this place, binding his word to Apollo's prediction. He prays to the Eumenides to accept him and to grant him some "great consummation" at the *katastrophē* (103), for his and Apollo's sake. "Don't treat me or

Apollo unfairly," he begs (86). He recognizes that his own promise is now bound up with Apollo's promise, each depending on the other. This characterization of the divine sign is fundamental in this play. Here the oracle and its fulfillment are presented as neither "mysterious" nor "fatal" for Oedipus; rather, they represent the common discourse of two speakers of the same language. In the *Iliad*, Hector tries to demystify the divine sign by exposing its conventionality, but for Oedipus in this play that very conventionality signifies his alliance with the gods, as he affirms the sign and declares his willingness to complete his side of the "agreement." There is no magic in this, but simply the power of the promise.

Although Oedipus recognizes that this is his predicted place of rest, he can only repeat the prophecy without understanding how it may be fulfilled.[6] He does not yet see how he shall find his rest or how he may become a blessing to Athens and a curse to Thebes. He can only attest to the firmness of his promise to stay in accordance with Apollo's oracle. Ismene's intervention to report the most recent prophecies concerning Oedipus enlightens him as to his role and poses a possible contradiction to Apollo's earlier prediction. The god's older oracle preordained Oedipus's death in Attica, in the Eumenides' grove, but the new oracles suggest an alternative future for Oedipus. Ismene tells Oedipus that the Oracle has said that Oedipus will be much sought after by Thebes, for he will be a *charis* ("grace" or "blessing") to them, alive or dead (389–90). Further, Apollo has said that if Thebes does not succeed in bringing Oedipus back, there will be a heavy curse on the Cadmeans, when they take their stand on his tomb (409–11). Ismene tells Oedipus that Creon himself, knowing the oracle, is coming to return Oedipus to be buried on Thebes' border. By this action he means to bring *charis* to Thebes, as the oracle

---

6. As Knox remarks, at this point Oedipus "speaks with blind faith in the prophecy": Bernard Knox, *The Heroic Temper: Studies in Sophoclean Tragedy* (Berkeley: University of California Press, 1964), p. 150.

said, and to avert the curse, while avoiding the pollution of Oedipus's presence within the city itself.

This prophecy, in contrast to the older oracle, seems to offer an alternative for the future. It is formulated as an either-or proposition, which, as David Grene says, makes Oedipus's plan "an either-or chance, which may succeed or fail."[7] It seems possible that Oedipus may not die in the Eumenides' grove if Creon can persuade him to return home. It will fall to Creon, and later, to Polynices, to bring about this interpretation of the newer oracle and thus to contravene Oedipus's reading of the oracles and make him renege on the promise he has made never to leave Attica.

In this conflict, Oedipus's presence and his word become the all-important focus of the action. The fulfillment of Apollo's original oracle depends on Oedipus's conscious decision to stay, while both Creon and Polynices need Oedipus's word of assent and his presence to make their own interpretation of the new oracle come true. From Oedipus's perspective, of course, the new and old oracles do not necessarily contradict each other. Knox describes that perspective as resulting in a choice: "Gradually it becomes clear that the new prophecy supplements the old.... He sees now that the two prophecies are one; it is by his choice of a resting place that he can do what Apollo promised him the power to do, to hurt his enemies and help his friends. He chooses to give victory to Athens and defeat to Thebes when one day Theban armies invade Attic soil."[8] What Oedipus "chooses" here is, in fact, what he has already decided to do: to remain in Attica, in the grove where Apollo had promised him rest and power. In other words, what he really chooses is to try to keep his word, with the knowledge that there may indeed be an alternative. That Oedipus has chosen, however, is not enough in these circumstances, for he alone,

7. David Grene, *Reality and the Heroic Pattern: Last Plays of Ibsen, Shakespeare, and Sophocles* (Chicago: University of Chicago Press, 1967), p. 156.
8. Knox, *Heroic Temper*, pp. 150–51.

physically helpless, cannot prevent Creon from forcing him to return to Thebes. It appears that there is still no "magic" or absolute guarantee in either Apollo's or Oedipus's word in the face of Creon's violent assault.

The Creon of *Antigone* first appears as the defender of the city and its values and yet proves to be an enemy to them in the end. From the beginning of this play, however, Creon represents a threat to Oedipus, to Athens, and to Apollo himself, as he undermines the culture and language that hold together man and man, and man and god, in their alliances.[9] His attempt to persuade Oedipus to return to Thebes and his subsequent seizure of the exile's daughters violate both the city's principles and Apollo's design. His success in removing Oedipus would invalidate the latter's promise and contradict Apollo's older oracle, which predicted that Oedipus should find his rest in the Eumenides' grove. On a more fundamental level, Creon's violence undermines the basic structures of civilized order: the sanctity of ritual, the law of suppliants, sanctions against violent crime, and the order of language itself, the order in the correspondence of speech and action (*logos* and *ergon*), which is the convention that ensures the fulfillment of both the divine and the human word.[10]

Oedipus himself describes Creon as one who breaks the bond between word and deed, violating the rules of normal language. He deplores Creon's disguising his cruelty with gentle speech, "sweetly speaking harsh words" (774). Creon impairs the conventional relationship between speech and action when his advances are "noble in word, but evil in deed" (*logō[i] men esthla, toisi d'ergoisin kaka*, 782).[11] Creon would break his own prom-

---

9. According to Segal, Creon here is a "perverter of civilized values" (p. 379).

10. In this discussion of Theseus and Creon, and the general topic of speech and silence in *Oedipus at Colonus*, I am indebted to Georgia Nugent and her paper on "Speech and Silence in the *Oedipus Coloneus*," delivered at the American Philological Association, annual meeting, San Francisco, 1981.

11. See also Segal, pp. 398–99, on *logos* and *ergon*.

ises, and his actions threaten to force Oedipus and Apollo to break theirs. Because Creon's violence would prevent the fulfillment of Apollo's oracle and Oedipus's vow to remain in Attica, the reliability of all promises—oracular or human—becomes suspect. Here the conventional relationship between word and deed is the basis of human interaction, whereas in the epic, convention is associated with the god's arbitrary imposition of meaning.

When the moment of crisis comes, when Oedipus and the Chorus seem incapable of resisting Creon's attack, it is Theseus, the mythical king of Athens and representative of civilization,[12] who restores order. His appearance here should be no surprise, for at the time of the play's composition, Athens was on the brink of its fall to Sparta. This Theseus is a composite fantasy of great leadership and advocacy of the principles of the democratic state, a kind of model king.[13] As the leader of Athens, he is thus in Sophocles' play clearly the answer to the tyrants who ruled in the earlier Theban plays and to the Theban Creon here. Theseus is not only a powerful leader who has the physical means to restore Oedipus's daughters and protect the old man from Creon, but unlike Creon, he is also a man who keeps his promises. He is a protector of the *nomoi*, "conventions," of both government and language. For instance, the Athenian king insists to Oedipus that deeds are more important to him than words: "It is not through words that I would have my life valued; rather I would make it shine through deeds" (1143–44). Yet when words are used, it is most important that the words and the deeds correspond. Thus when Theseus promises

12. As Knox reminds us in his introduction to *Oedipus at Colonus*, Theseus was the "mythic founder of the unity of Attica under the city of Athens": see *Sophocles: The Three Theban Plays*, trans. Robert Fagles (New York: Viking, 1982), p. 247. On the ideological difference between Athens and Thebes in this play and elsewhere, see Froma I. Zeitlin, "Thebes: Theater of Self and Society in Athenian Drama," in *Greek Tragedy and Political Theory*, ed. J. Peter Euben (Berkeley: University of California Press, 1986), pp. 101–41.

13. Gilberte Ronnet, *Sophocle, poète tragique* (Paris: Boccard, 1969), p. 292.

to settle Oedipus in Athens in return for his blessing, Oedipus presses him to keep that vow, saying that he will never bind Theseus with an oath, as if Theseus were not to be trusted (650). Theseus replies that he can give no more than with his word (651). The king thus emphasizes that he does not need to swear before the gods to guarantee his promise. He needs no supernatural power to enforce his word, and throughout the play he emphasizes that he has indeed kept that word. Similarly, when Theseus restores Oedipus's daughters to him, he reminds Oedipus that he has not lied to him (1145–46). When Oedipus is afraid that Polynices, too, may take him away, Theseus renews his pledge (1209), and his last gift to Oedipus is to swear again never to forsake Oedipus's daughters or to reveal his resting place. Both Apollo and Oedipus need Theseus, the secular leader, not just for his ability to act or for his military power but also for his word, which, along with Oedipus's word, is bound to the oracles of Apollo.

The role of Theseus emphasizes the importance of the promise in the play, as the secular complement to the oracle as a form of prediction. Apollo's oracle, affirmed by Oedipus, cannot be realized in this play without Theseus's fulfillment of his promise. The secular bond of faith—not an oath sworn before a god—here sustains and verifies the god's words or "promise." In a reversal of Oedipus's position in *Oedipus the King*, Theseus acts as the keeper of the civic order, as its benevolent and effective leader, and as the one who ensures the divine order and the fulfillment of oracles through the realization of his own words. It is important that we recognize that the play thus presents no "magic" or mystery in the fulfillment of the oracle that Oedipus shall die in Attica; it is accomplished through Oedipus's resolve and Theseus's might and reliability.

The second half of the play, however, also confirms the power of human language in its representation of the power of the curse, the dark side and "magic" of the human word. Even as Theseus reunites Oedipus with his daughters and Creon departs, Theseus introduces Oedipus to his last antagonist,

Polynices, whom he must fight alone. Polynices has come to ask Oedipus to forsake Athens, return with him, and give up his anger and revoke his old curse on his sons. Again, Oedipus's acceding to this supplication would invalidate both Apollo's oracle and his own words, but this time Oedipus does not need Theseus or Apollo to protect him. Unlike the episode with Creon, Oedipus's episode with Polynices focuses on the immediate future of Oedipus's family, that is, the coming war between the exiled Polynices and his younger brother Eteocles.[14] When Oedipus early on in the play discovers that his sons, knowing Apollo's latest oracles, have made no attempt to bring him back, he prays that he may be the one (*en d'emoi telos*) to determine their future in battle (422–23), for then Eteocles, who holds the throne, would not last, and Polynices, who is in exile, would not return (425–26). It is the very absence of this subject from Apollo's oracle which suggests that Oedipus alone has the potential to speak for his sons' future.[15] As the play's action begins to move out of the realms of both Apollo's and Theseus's control and into Oedipus's sphere, Oedipus speaks not promises and vows, the discourse of civilization, but curses, a primeval binding language.

When Polynices does come to bring him back, Oedipus recognizes that this is his moment to speak of the future. The scene with Polynices establishes the independence of Oedipus's voice from Apollo's authority, through his power to speak curses. Up to this point, Oedipus has been, in effect, Apollo's prophet, in that he speaks in Apollo's name when he speaks of the future.[16] When he tells Theseus of the strife to come

14. Sophocles has revised certain aspects of the story as we know it from epic fragments and from Aeschylus's *Seven Against Thebes* and Euripides' *Phoenician Women*, particularly the relationship between the two brothers, the nature of Oedipus's curse, and Oedipus's fate after the discovery of his identity.

15. Knox (*Heroic Temper*, p. 151) comments that "the punishment of his ingrate sons is something over which the prophecy gives him no control, and that he can express only as a wish, a prayer."

16. Knox, *Heroic Temper*, p. 156.

between Athens and Thebes (something Theseus cannot foresee), he speaks from his own experience of mutability, but he
also defers to the Olympians' authority. These things will happen, he says, if "Zeus is still Zeus, and Phoebus Apollo is clear
[*saphēs*]" (623). After rejecting Creon's cajolery, Oedipus pronounces a savage curse on Thebes itself and hints at his sons'
deaths (783–90), but again he calls on Apollo and Zeus when
he claims his superior knowledge of Thebes' condition and
future. He taunts Creon with this superiority, saying, "Don't
I know the truth about Thebes better than you? So much better,
for those I heed are wiser, Apollo and his father Zeus" (791–
93). Like Tiresias in the earlier plays, Oedipus says he can
speak of the future because Apollo has revealed it to him. Like
the blind prophet, the blind Oedipus, who submits in the present to his child's guidance, can see the future with Apollo's
eyes.

When Oedipus curses his sons in response to Polynices' pleas,
however, he speaks not as a Tiresias or a servant of Apollo.
Interpreting Apollo's new oracle to mean that Oedipus will
bring victory to whatever brother he aids in the coming war,
Polynices begs Oedipus to return with him. Oedipus, provoked
to anger by his son's late repentance, pronounces another future
for the brothers. When Oedipus predicts that Polynices will
never win victory over Thebes and that he and his brother will
fall, stained with each other's blood, Oedipus does so remembering "those curses [*aras*] against both of you which I spoke
before" (1375). In what appears to be a reference to the epic
version of his earlier curse on his sons,[17] Oedipus emphasizes
that he is now repeating a curse that *he* made long ago. Like
Apollo's oracle, Oedipus's curse is a "prediction" spoken long
before, which Oedipus takes up again; in this case, however,
the past and present word belong to Oedipus alone.

17. There is, of course, great controversy over the meaning of l. 1375. See
Knox, *Heroic Temper*, p. 194, n.14. The epic version of the curse can be
found in *Thebais*, fr. 2, in T. W. Allen, *Homeri Opera*, vol. 5.

Earlier in the play, Oedipus had revived Apollo's old prophecy in order to determine his own future; here he repeats and validates his own words, which speak of the future. The curse, like the promise, is a form of speaking the future as prophecy does, but the promise involves a conventional agreement or bond between two parties, while the curse is meant to impose a future. The curse works through belief and "magic," unlike the promise, which is upheld by custom and law. In this sense, Oedipus's curse imitates prophecy as it is typically conceived in that the word is thought not just to represent but also to make the future. That Oedipus's curse is understood as prophecy becomes clear in the exchange between his children which follows his diatribe. Antigone reproaches Polynices for proceeding willingly into the doom that Oedipus has "prophesied" (*manteumath'*, 1425); in her words, he has spoken oracles (*ethespisen*, 1428).[18] But here he does not rely on Zeus's or Apollo's revelation to support him; instead he depends on the existence of Dikē, or Justice, to ratify his claim, and on the power of his curses to *make* the future.[19]

Many scholars, certainly, have seen that here at last Oedipus is presented as a prophet in his own right through his power to curse.[20] Yet few stress the analogy between this scene and the earlier scenes of the protagonist's confrontation with the prophet, especially that of Oedipus and Tiresias in *Oedipus the King*.[21] In *Oedipus at Colonus*, if Oedipus takes on the role of prophet, his son Polynices acts the hero's part, as once again the "hero" and "prophet" are divided by the prophet's silence—a silence like that of the gods themselves. In *Oedipus the King*, the prophet's silence is implicit, as Tiresias speaks at

18. See Peter Burian, "Suppliant and Saviour: *Oedipus at Colonus*," *Phoenix* 28 (1974): 425, on Oedipus's "prophecy."

19. Knox, *Heroic Temper*, p. 160: "He both foresees and determines the future."

20. See Knox, *Heroic Temper*, pp. 144, 160; Segal, pp. 384–85; Burian, pp. 425–26.

21. Segal and Seidensticker have noted some of the analogies.

least to indicate that he has a secret. In this scene, however, at first Oedipus will not speak at all. When Polynices humbles himself before his father and then craves his blessing, Oedipus says nothing. The son then begs the father to speak, and when the old man is silent, asks his sister to try to move "the un-approachable and silent mouth" of Oedipus (1277). Antigone advises Polynices to speak again, for words can move a man and "give a voice to the mute" (*paresche phōnēn tois aphō-nētois tina*, 1283). When Polynices appeals again, however, Oedipus appears untouched by pity. When he does answer, only at the Chorus's request, it is with a fury that far exceeds Tiresias's anger when he is provoked by Oedipus to speak the truth at last; here, Oedipus outdoes Tiresias in both speech and silence.

Polynices' behavior in this scene recalls both Oedipus in the earlier play and Creon in *Antigone*. Segal has described the exchange between Polynices and Antigone as a "miniature So-phoclean tragedy," in which "the doomed hero is unshakable in his violent resolve and his self-destructive passions and a loving woman tries to call him back to life."[22] We can also say that this exchange replays earlier Sophoclean protagonists'— and epic heroes'—responses to prophecy. In *Antigone*, Creon submits himself to an inflexible fate through his own inflexi-bility, even as he believes that he forestalls that fate. The younger Oedipus brings about the "fated" revelation of the truth through his own stubborn search for it. But Polynices, more than either of them, brings about the disaster prophesied by Oedipus through his own fatalism. At first this exchange seems close to Hector's response to Polydamas in *Iliad* 12. After Oedipus speaks, Antigone acts as a kind of *mantis*, a Polydamas to Polynices' Hector, when she begs Polynices to turn back his army to keep Oedipus's oracle from coming true. Polynices rejects her counsel, saying that he cannot turn back now: he could never raise such an army again, and he must attack

22. Segal, p. 389.

Thebes, for "flight is shameful" (*aischron to pheugein*, 1422).
These are words that clearly echo Hector's reply to Polydamas,
when he refuses to turn back to Troy. Unlike Hector, however,
while Polynices refuses Antigone's counsel, he never denies the
power of Oedipus's curse, as Hector denies the significance of
the bird sign.[23] Polynices cannot see any choice for himself, as
Hector does. He believes that what is to come is in the hands
of the *daimōn*, "destiny" (1443–44). Polynices may, for a moment, question Oedipus's knowledge of the future, but at the
same time he testifies that an external power, not his own voice,
governs his life.[24]

While Polynices lacks Hector's skepticism, he also falls short
of the prophetic vision of the dying Hector—and of the aged
Oedipus. Segal has called Polynices a younger Oedipus,[25] one
who ignores others' prophetic warnings and plunges ahead to
disaster. But he stands in contrast to the Oedipus of this play.
Polynices is motivated by a fear of shame, a heroic value that
seems outdated here. The Oedipus of *Oedipus at Colonus* has
already experienced the deepest shame. He has seen prophecy
fulfilled. But he does more than just piously affirm Apollo's
oracles; in recognizing the truth of oracular language, he imitates and exceeds it in his ferocity against his sons. He seizes

23. Some readers interpret Polynices' response to Antigone as his ready
submission to the doom of which his father has spoken. Reinhardt, with
Whitman, sees Polynices as really responsible for his own disaster; he contrasts
him with Eteocles in Aeschylus's *Seven Against Thebes*: "In Aeschylus, the
hero suffers a *god*-given fate, but Polynices succumbs to the confusion and
complexity of *human* errors, limitations, and mistakes, and is dragged away
in their clutches." See Karl Reinhardt, *Sophocles*, trans. H. Harvey and D.
Harvey (New York: Barnes & Noble, 1979), p. 218. See also Whitman, p.
211: "By the time Oedipus utters his curse, Polyneices is already on his way
to the war, and is too fatally involved to turn back, as his words to Antigone
show."

24. See R. P. Winnington-Ingram, *Sophocles: An Interpretation* (Cambridge: Cambridge University Press, 1980), chap. 11, on Oedipus's reliance
not on the Olympian gods but on chthonic powers—especially the Furies and
the justice they uphold.

25. Segal, p. 384.

on the power of the curse as his own way of speaking the future. As to Hector, this prophetic power comes to Oedipus as he hesitates on the boundary between the world of the living and the world of the dead. It is by dying that Oedipus gains demonic power to help the Athenians and harm the Thebans, and the imminence of his death seems to evoke that power.[26] When he speaks of the future at the end, he does not necessarily speak by divine sanction;[27] Oedipus is independent of the gods, while joined with them. When summoned by the gods' thunder to prepare for his death, Oedipus walks not like the prophet Tiresias, with the help of a guide, but by himself. In the same way he no longer needs the voice of the god to speak for or through him when he speaks of the future.

Oedipus's demonic power, however, raises the same ethical problems that Hector's story raises, when the costs of heroic defiance are added up. In some ways, Oedipus harks back to the Creon of *Antigone*, who desired the kind of near divinity and power of fatality that Oedipus himself possesses in this play. Critics disagree, certainly, about Oedipus's "humanity" in the scene with Polynices. For some, his curse is demonic and his terrible justice is more divine than human. It is not what we recognize as justice at all, but is more like the "justice" of the gods in *Oedipus the King*. His vengefulness against his sons shocks those expecting a passive and pious old man. Peter Burian describes Oedipus's curse as "standing outside the boundaries of ordinary moral judgment,"[28] and Bowra tries hard to justify Oedipus's wrath against Polynices on the grounds of ordinary morality, but he, too, concludes that "Oedipus moves in a different world and exercises the power of a

---

26. Ronnet remarks: "His imminent death which makes this power effective surrounds him like a kind of sacred prestige, as if he were in communication with the gods, as if he were himself a god" (p. 308, translation mine).

27. See Reinhardt, p. 219; also Segal, p. 405.

28. Burian, p. 427, citing R. P. Winnington-Ingram, "A Religious Function of Greek Tragedy: A Study in the *Oedipus Coloneus* and the *Oresteia*," *Journal of Hellenic Studies* 74 (1954): 24. See also Grene, p. 165.

daemon."[29] Yet at the same time, we must recognize the Oedipus of the Messenger's speech at the end, the Oedipus who expresses tenderness and pity for his daughters. This is a father who repays his children with love, who is the antithesis of the father who cursed Polynices. In this contradictory mix of demonic power and human *ēthos*, we see that Oedipus has radically revised the model of Hector, hero of family and city, which seems so basic to the portrayal of his younger self.

In *Oedipus at Colonus*, Oedipus stands between god and man as a hero quite different from the Homeric hero. Oedipus's heroism redefines the opposition between the sacred and secular created in the defiance of prophecy. If in fifth-century Athens the realms of the secular and sacred were thought to be contiguous and allied, the tragic defiance of prophecy forces the sacred and secular apart. Hector must contradict god and prophet in order to speak for himself and his city. Similarly, Oedipus in *Oedipus the King* believes that human stories discredit oracles as a means of interpreting events, and Creon in *Antigone* opposes secular necessity to divine authority, while coveting that inhuman authority for himself. In *Oedipus at Colonus*, however, the hero begins by identifying his words with the god's prediction when he becomes Apollo's prophet and even when he speaks for himself. In the end, while still very much a father, brutal and loving, he assumes a god's place in the silence of the sacred grove of the Eumenides.

Oedipus at Colonus also differs from the earlier plays and from epic in its portrayal of the hero's role in the city. Both *Antigone* and *Oedipus the King* show how the city is disrupted by those who imitate the epic models of behavior, particularly the model of Hector's defiance. *Antigone* emphasizes the political consequences of imitating Hector's defiance in the democratic city. Creon, in asserting his voice as the city's in contradiction of god and prophet, becomes a negative model, the paradigm of the tyrant. When Antigone, a woman, defies

29. Bowra, pp. 328–30.

this new "god" in defense of the *agrapta nomima*, she threatens the city's security while she affirms its oldest customs. In *Oedipus the King*, Sophocles combines Antigone and Creon into one hero, Oedipus, who is at once the city's defender and its enemy, the source of its disaster. Oedipus's defiance of the prophet, his attempt to explain human events in human terms, is to be both admired and criticized. It celebrates human reason and freedom of speech, which are the democratic city's foundation, yet it also undermines the god's assurance of civic order, as represented in the fulfillment of oracles. In both plays, the hero's role as the city's leader presents irreconcilable contradictions: Creon's behavior threatens democracy, while Oedipus's defiance destabilizes the order guaranteed by oracles, at whatever cost. Yet at the same time their actions are based on values the democratic city is designed to preserve—loyalty to community and freedom of conviction. In *Oedipus at Colonus*, however, Oedipus, with all his crimes, is accepted by Athens as its protector and at the same time is embraced in the end by the gods themselves in a way that seems to violate all precedents for Sophocles' representation of the hero's relationship to the city.

In *Oedipus at Colonus*, Sophocles overcomes the problems posed by the model of epic defiance of prophecy by identifying Oedipus with hero-cult, in contrast to the epic heroism of his son Polynices. Knox, Meautis, and other scholars emphasize that the attribution of supernatural beneficent and destructive powers to Oedipus's grave marks him as a hero of cult—a once great or terrible man, now dead, who must be granted propitiatory sacrifice.[30] Though we do not know in the end how much of Sophocles' story of Oedipus's heroization is of his own

---

30. On hero-cult in general, see. L. R. Farnell, *Greek Hero-Cults and Ideas of Immortality* (Oxford: Clarendon, 1921); and Angelo Brelich, *Gli eroi greci: un problema storico-religioso* (Rome: Ateneo, 1958). On Oedipus, tragedy, and hero-cult, see Knox, *Heroic Temper*, chaps. 1 and 2; George Meautis, *"L'Oedipe à Colone" et le culte des héros* (Neuchâtel: Secretariat à l'Université, 1946).

invention,[31] there is some historical evidence to indicate that a cult of Oedipus did exist in Attica: Pausanius records a hero-cult of Oedipus and Adrastus at Colonus, which maintained Oedipus's sepulchral monument on the Areopagus, in the precinct of the Furies' shrine.[32] In his study of the vocabulary of heroism in the *Iliad*, Gregory Nagy notes an essential difference between the epic and cult hero: the hero of cult is associated with an individual *polis* and is considered its defender, whereas the epic hero is Panhellenic.[33] Further, the cult hero did not come into conflict with the gods. Homeric epic, says Nagy, displays a ritual antagonism between god and hero which is never reconciled, as the great heroes meet their death at the gods' hands and find immortality not among the blessed in Elysium or on Olympus but only in human memory. In hero-cult, however, the hero is a mortal transformed into a being with supernatural powers, owed the sacrifice and reverence due to a god. When an epic hero becomes, in time, a hero of cult, he gains more than *kleos*; he gains a place among the gods, while still in a mortal grave in the earth.

It is in this sense that Sophocles redefines Oedipus's heroism by giving him a hero-cult. Oedipus finds a place of rest, where he can be the city's defender for all time, not as its leader but as a kind of god. When he confronts and rejects Polynices, Oedipus dissociates himself from the form of tragic heroism that Polynices acts out, a heroism in which the hero is driven to destroy his city and himself, turning his face from its gods. The very violence and affront to the principles of civilization that Oedipus's past represents are incorporated to constitute a power by which the city can defend itself. Thus the city has

31. See Knox, intro. to *Oedipus at Colonus*, p. 238.

32. Farnell suspects, however, that this monument may have post-dated Sophocles' play, being inspired by its legend rather than suggesting its theme (p. 333, citing Pausanius 1.30.4; 28.6).

33. Gregory Nagy, *The Best of the Achaeans: Concepts of the Hero in Archaic Greek Poetry* (Baltimore: Johns Hopkins University Press, 1979), pp. 114–15.

found a way to bring both criminal and god into its service, through the terms of hero-cult. When Hector dies, he assumes a prophetic voice and godlike understanding, but purely on his own terms, as he never ceases to see the gods as his antagonists. Oedipus, in the end, both accepts and embodies divinity.

One striking feature of Sophocles' version of Oedipus's cult distinguishes it from the typical hero-cult, however: Oedipus's insistence that Theseus never reveal the location of his grave. As Bowra notes, "such circumstances are unusual. A hero's grave was usually known and was the place where he was honored."[34] It was a place of public worship, at once a sign of his difference from the gods, who have no graves, and the locus and source of his superhuman powers. But Oedipus stresses repeatedly that his grave must be secret. He asks Theseus, "Never tell it to any man, do not even indicate the neighborhood where it lies" (1522–23), for then it shall remain a greater protection for them than the many spears or shields of friends. Even Oedipus's daughters are excluded from the knowledge of its location. They may not see what is unlawful to see or hear what cannot be rightly spoken (1641–42). Theseus must remind them that Oedipus said that "no one must go near that place, nor any mortal should speak in that sacred grove" (1761–63). Oedipus thus passes at last into that silence he cursed upon himself in *Oedipus the King*. At the end of the earlier play, Oedipus does not hide in silence, but shows himself to the city and speaks his pain, bringing what should be hidden and secret to light and to speech. In *Oedipus at Colonus*, however, an existence in silence and secrecy is not anathema to the hero; it is his desired *telos* and the token of his power.

Oedipus's end in silence and secrecy marks a fundamental difference between the definition of heroism in *Oedipus at Colonus* and that in the earlier Theban plays. In *Antigone*,

---

34. Bowra, p. 341. Bowra does note that "at Thebes only the ruler knew where was the grave of Dirce (Plutarch, *Gen. Soc.* 5)." See also Segal, pp. 482–83, nn. 31, 43.

Antigone's heroism consists of her determination to act independently and openly and to speak her mind. As she proceeds to her living tomb in the desert, she commands attention by speaking of her sorrow and her pride, and she dies rather than suffer living silence.

In *Oedipus the King*, Oedipus attempts to break the silence of prophet and citizen alike with his own free and open speech. In the earlier play, Oedipus construes silence as something external to himself, subversive to his will, a sign of tyranny—yet he cannot hear the unspoken meanings in his own words, as later he cannot recognize his own tyranny. Although in his own curse he condemns himself to silence, the play gives him a free and apostrophic speech in disaster, as he moves out of the city's jurisdiction.

In *Oedipus at Colonus*, however, Oedipus is portrayed as a hero who commands both speech and silence, on the the city's margins, in defense of Athens and for the destruction of Thebes. In the scene with Polynices, Oedipus's independence and authority are voiced in his curse, which has the power to destroy his sons. In his death, Oedipus's power is guarded by silence, secure in the secret grove. If, as Whitman has said, *Oedipus at Colonus* is a story of Oedipus's "battle for significance,"[35] the significance he obtains is that of a hermetic sign, like the oracle, which both reveals and conceals, potent in its very obscurity. In *Oedipus the King*, silence belongs to the gods, while speech is the province of humans, particularly Oedipus. In *Oedipus at Colonus*, not only does a man embrace silence, but the gods come to speak to the hero, in their own voice and in the first person. When Oedipus lingers too long on the threshold of death, they call to him as to one of them: "Why do we wait to move?" (1627–28). Here, as the gods find speech, Oedipus discovers silence and a divinity which, like the silence in his own speech, is not external or autocratic but within himself.

At the same time, we cannot forget that this divinity is as-

35. Whitman, p. 198.

serted in Oedipus's fury against his sons and the city of Thebes. Demonic power has not been ethically transformed in Oedipus's new silences and words. The demonic sign has been integrated with the human voice to serve the community of Athens as a kind of protective magic. But this language is still characterized as magic, belying the importance placed on convention, law, and promises earlier in the play. In Homeric epic and the earlier Theban plays, the defiance of prophecy both subverts and ultimately confirms the essential amorality of prophetic authority. So, too, in *Oedipus at Colonus*, the mystery of the gods' power is ultimately protected. The story of Hector suggests that the impulse to reject or subvert prophecy affirms ethical values in the face of the gods' impassive interest in plot. As Heraclitus observed, "To the gods, all things are beautiful; human beings, however, hold some things right and others wrong."[36] But Hector's story, like the stories of Creon and Antigone and Oedipus, also suggests that the power of plotting is as irresistible to people as it is to the gods. These characters may begin by writing their own stories, but their stories belong to everyone, not to themselves alone, and so to take possession of them eventually amounts to an act of tyranny. Sophocles, in the end, could never accept the power of storytelling as anything less than godlike, safe only in the hands of divinity or spoken in the anonymous and collective voice of myth.

36. Heraclitus 102, in H. Diels, *Die Fragmente der Vorsokratiker*, 7th ed. (Berlin: Weidmann, 1954).

Euripides and the Erasure of Prophecy

We should not be surprised that Sophocles did not permit Oedipus to escape his story. Aristotle observed, a bit disapprovingly, that the tragedians still clung to the "historically given names" and the stories associated with them, for "what has happened is...possible" and "what is possible is persuasive."[1] Yet I have suggested that Sophocles comes closer than we may think to questioning the authority of such stories and of the oracles that shape them. This is an observation more commonly made about Euripides, whose skeptical attitude toward myth, as well as oracles and prophecies, is well known. Euripides pushed his characters to the limits of the "historical" boundaries,[2] just as he persistently questioned the role of or-

1. Aristotle, *Poetics* 1451b1; I use here the translation of Gerald F. Else (Ann Arbor: University of Michigan Press, 1967; rpt. 1970), p. 33. Aristotle notes the exception of Agathon's *Antheus*, among others, in which the names are "as fictional as the events."

2. See R. P. Winnington-Ingram, "Euripides: *Poiêtes Sophos*," *Arethusa* 2 (1969): 127–42, esp. 132–33. See also Froma I. Zeitlin, "The Closet of Masks: Role-Playing and Myth-Making in the *Orestes* of Euripides," *Ramus* 9 (1980): 51–77, for a brilliant discussion of Euripides' play with myth and fiction in the *Orestes*: "While the new plot struggles to accommodate itself to the changed circumstances which prompted its invention in the first place, it both marks a radical break with the mythic tradition and, at the same time, asserts the irresistibility of the mythic paradigm" (p. 52).

acles and signs in governing human lives. I believe that Sophocles and Euripides shared similar views of the political and dramatic function of prophecy, views based on their familiarity with the uses of prophecy in Athenian society and politics, as well as in its literature. Euripides' versions of Theban prophets and kings in the *Bacchae* and *Phoenissae* and his echoing of Oedipus's story in his *Ion* suggest that he, like Sophocles, was aware that prophecy was a powerful form of fiction making in their world. Unlike the older poet, however, Euripides did not always protect the mystery of such fictions. As Cedric Whitman remarks, Euripides "constantly reminds his audience that he is making what they see before them, whereas the two earlier poets [Sophocles and Aeschylus] foster the illusion that the mythic tale is creating or recreating itself."[3] A brief glance at Euripides' experimentation with divine signs and human voices, oracles and *mythoi*, reveals that Sophocles and Euripides shared a culture that respected and yet questioned prophecy, and that Euripides took the kinds of questions that Sophocles implicitly raised about the abuse of prophecy and brought them to the surface in his own plays, exposing the mysteries of oracular authority.

Euripides' reputation as a debunker of religion, including prophecy and oracles, was so relentlessly expounded in the earlier part of this century that a reaction has necessarily set in.[4] Attention has been drawn again to his role as a dramatist rather than as a philosopher, to temper our concern with his rationalism.[5] Yet I have contended that what we call "dramatic

3. Cedric H. Whitman, *Euripides and the Full Circle of Myth* (Cambridge: Harvard University Press, 1974), p. 114.

4. That reputation was established in A. W. Verrall's *Euripides the Rationalist* (Cambridge: Cambridge University Press, 1895). For an early statement on Euripides and prophecy, see L. Radermacher, "Euripides und die Mantik," *Rheinisches Museum für Philologie* 53 (1898): 497–510.

5. For two different versions see Winnington-Ingram, "Euripides," who focuses on the idea of Euripides' "cleverness," and G. M. A. Grube, who writes that "in the search for Euripides the rationalist, the idealist, the iconclast and the rest, Euripides the dramatist is almost forgotten": *The Drama of*

technique" has philosophical or ideological significance, just as ideas themselves have a dramatic character. This is particularly true in the case of dramatic and political prophecy, in which the terms of religion, politics, and drama cannot easily be separated. It is thus precisely through study of Euripides' "dramatic technique," especially his use of oracles, that we can apprehend his ideas about the role of the gods in our lives.

Recently scholars concerned with Euripides' criticism of prophecy and oracles have focused on his plays associated with the myths of Orestes (*Electra*, *Iphigenia in Tauris*, and *Orestes*), all of which involve the representation of Apollo and his oracle in history as well as in the constellation of myths revolving around the house of Atreus. These readers have drawn attention to the pressures of the myth, the forced endings, and the problematic morality of the oracles of Apollo in these plays.[6] Here I focus on Euripides' working out of paradigms associated more closely with Thebes than with Argos—that is, his portraits of Tiresias in the *Phoenissae* and *Bacchae* and, at greater length, his *Ion*, which has an uncanny resemblance to *Oedipus the King*.[7] The Theban and Argive models concerning Apollo are

---

Euripides (London: Methuen, 1941; rpt. New York: Barnes & Noble, 1973), p. 10. See also T. B. L. Webster, *The Tragedies of Euripides* (London: Methuen, 1967): "The traditional stories may be untrue, they may or may not be paradeigmatic, but they are immortal, and they may be beautiful. Euripides is too good a poet to abandon them" (p. 292).

6. Deborah H. Roberts, *Apollo and His Oracle in the "Oresteia"* (Goettingen: Vandenhoeck & Ruprecht, 1984), chap. 5, provides an excellent discussion of Euripidean variations on the Orestes story in these plays and of the idea of ending or closure: "In the *Electra*, he attacks the tradition that there is justice in what Apollo commands, but retains in some respects the traditional ending. In the *Iphigenia in Tauris*, the Aeschylean ending is undone and the suffering prolonged; a happy ending is finally reached but the god's grandeur has been diminished. In the *Orestes*, Euripides turns in the end to irony, the only possible weapon against a god who, deprived of justice and majesty, still retains power over plots" (p. 120). Zeitlin discusses Euripides' reading of Orestes trying to remake his own myth in the *Orestes*. It is also useful to look at Euripides' representation of Polymestor in *Hecuba* as a severely compromised figure who comes to prophesy at the play's end.

7. The similarity has been noted by Whitman, pp. 78–79, especially that both plays are about the quest for parentage and the quest for knowledge.

essentially different, though they are related. Orestes' story always focuses on his choosing to carry out Apollo's command that he murder his mother, a command that leads one to question the god's role as an agent in human justice. Oedipus's and Creon's stories, however, are organized around the defiance or avoidance of oracles that predict the future. The distinction between a prediction and a command is, of course, a crucial one, in terms of the problems of authority and speech investigated here. But it can be said that Orestes' story, in all its versions, dramatizes the act of obeying the oracle as a means of shaping a self, whereas the Theban heroes' stories represent defiance as a way of self-fashioning. Thus unlike Sophocles, Euripides was not much interested in exploring the tradition of the heroic individual. As Whitman puts it, "throughout his life, Euripides made use of heroic fiction, without ever shaping a heroic figure."[8] Euripides' skeptical attitude toward the hero touches every kind of character in his plays, especially the figure of the hero's antitype, the prophet. In Euripides' plays, Tiresias, the hero's powerful antagonist in Sophocles' Theban plays, is as diminished a figure as any of his heroes. To echo Whitman, in fashioning Tiresias Euripides made use of prophetic fictions without ever really shaping a prophet.

In *Phoenissae*, the one play we have that deals directly with the house of Laius, both Oedipus and Tiresias are lesser men.[9] Unlike Sophocles' Oedipus, this Oedipus has not been exposed and led into exile; instead he is hidden inside the dark house, blind, to wail away his days (335–36). Having cursed his sons for imprisoning him, he now regrets and mourns his curses (334), repeatedly and futilely seeking death by his own hand. He has no faith in his words and no faith in himself. When he does appear, he is a shadow, a ghost, an unburied corpse, and a fleeting dream (1542–45). When Oedipus moans that he will fall where fate would have him, even his own daughter reacts

8. Whitman, p. 112.
9. Webster tells us of Euripides' lost *Oidipous*, "of which at least we know that Oidipous did not blind himself but was blinded by the retainers of Laios, and Iokaste remained loyal to him through everything" (p. 15).

with outrage. "Where," asks Antigone, "are Oedipus and his famous riddles?" Oedipus answers, "Destroyed" (1688–89). No longer skilled in reading riddles, he finds that even his own words fail him, for his curses are powerful in spite of him, not because he wills them to be so.

It is fitting that the Tiresias of *Phoenissae* never confronts this shadow Oedipus; rather, the prophet finds another familiar antagonist in the figure of Creon. Eteocles has sent Creon's son Menoeceus to fetch Tiresias; having himself alienated Tiresias, Eteocles asks Creon to speak to the seer, thus avoiding a possible heroic confrontation. Tiresias enters, aching with fatigue, and is guided with difficulty to a seat.[10] When Creon asks him how they might ensure the safety of their city, Tiresias offers two alternative plans. The first recommends that Oedipus' family be banished from the land; the second is another *mēchanē sōtērias* (890–93), or "saving plan," that he will not mention because it is a bitter *pharmakon* (which means both "poison" and "cure"). This reticence, of course, appears to evoke a familiar conflict between the prophet who will not speak to save the city and the ruler who will make him speak. But the sides are suddenly switched when Tiresias does speak, providing the second solution: sacrifice your son Menoeceus to appease Ares' rage for Cadmus's killing of the dragon, and your city will be saved. Then it is Creon who will not hear or listen (919). It is the king who asks for silence (925) and the prophet who refuses to hold his tongue (*ou siōpēsaimen an*, 926). In defending himself, Tiresias insists that it is for others to act, but for him to speak (*emoi d'eirēsetai*, 928). After clarifying the god's reason for the sacrifice, he asks to be taken home, complaining about the prophet's trade as an unpleasant and dangerous one; he leaves Creon in stricken silence, desperate for a way to save his son.

10. He is tired because he has just come from Athens, bearing a crown of victory for aiding them in war (bringing them to victory through the sacrifice of another child). Ironically, Creon takes that crown as a favorable *oiōnos* (858).

Two important modifications have been made to the confrontation between Tiresias and the king presented in Sophocles' Theban plays. Tiresias still emanates some of the power of his special knowledge, but his character is diminished. His physical frailties are emphasized, and the angry and stubborn seer of Sophocles is reduced to something of a whiner, who enters complaining about his feet and exits complaining about his job. The prophet's exchange with Creon also inverts the conventional opposition of prophetic silence and human speech. On the one hand, after Tiresias has spoken, Creon is the one who begs the prophet to keep silent; on the other hand, Tiresias admits that all he can do is speak, rather than *do* anything. Silence here is thus represented as craven rather than powerful, but just speaking itself is the easy way out, more cowardly than acting.

The other characters, especially Menoeceus, see Creon as lacking courage in his effort to avoid the prophecy. In fact, Creon's avoidance is not a proper defiance of prophecy at all because he accepts what Tiresias says. He has been given an either-or choice: either save your city or save your son. Creon is thus faced with a moral dilemma, a choice between duty to city and duty to family, rather than a heroic one.[11] But is Menoeceus's choice to kill himself heroic? It is not, insofar as it is a response to the prophecy. Menoeceus, too, accepts the prophet's terms completely and kills himself on the guarantee that his suicide will save the land. There may be heroism in self-sacrifice, but as one reader points out, by the end "the sacrifice itself appears again only as a pathetic incident (chiefly in Kreon's laments); its effect on the city's survival is given only the most casual mention."[12] The prophetic episode is not

11. Creon does say that he doesn't need Tiresias's prophesying, but Tiresias contemptuously replies: "Is the truth destroyed when you are unfortunate?" (922). Creon responds by falling on his knees to beg him to not say this to anyone else.

12. Introduction to Euripides, *The Phoenician Women*, trans. Peter Burian and Brian Swann (New York: Oxford University Press, 1981), p. 10.

central to the action and motivation of the play. Just as the former hero is a shadow and the prophet's voice is weakened, the structural role of prophecy collapses in this highly episodic play.[13]

Compared with the weak scenes of prophecy in *Phoenissae*, the confrontation between the hero Pentheus and the prophet Tiresias in the *Bacchae* has a better claim to being a heroic conflict resembling those in Sophocles' Theban plays. Pentheus reacts more violently than Oedipus or Creon ever do to Tiresias's long speech of advice. Like his predecessors, the young prince first accuses Tiresias of being interested only in profit, but then he directs his attendants to desecrate the prophet's shrine and the sacred objects within it. This may seem like stronger defiance than we have yet encountered, but its force is deflated when we realize that Tiresias never really prophesies. Commentators have insisted that Euripides is poking fun at Tiresias as well as Cadmus here—first, because it is ridiculous for old men to cavort in fawn skins as Bacchants do, and second, because Tiresias is portrayed as a Sophist, an incongruous identity for a *mantis*. In fact, it is something of a relief to see Tiresias for once not tired and impatient but bursting with energy, and that Pentheus thinks they look ridiculous does not mean we should think so. Further, Tiresias's resemblance to a Sophist is not necessarily incongruous. Paul Roth draws our attention to the "number of *manteis* active in the fifth and fourth centuries who were undoubtedly sympathetic towards, if not wholehearted participants in, the intellectual movements

---

13. J. C. Kamerbeek, "Prophecy and Tragedy," *Mnemosyne* 4 (1965): 29–40. As Kamerbeek says, "we do pity Creon, we do admire his son, but the scene does not strike us as touching the very roots of existence as does the fierce debate between Oedipus and Teiresias. It moves rather on a moral than on an existential plane" (p. 39). Kamerbeek points out further: "It is only logical that in proportion as *Tuchē*'s [Chance's] part in the dramatization of human destiny grows, the essential significance of oracles and prophecies is lessened, and as a matter of fact we hardly find in Euripides any scene of prophecy equal to the Cassandra-scene of Aeschylus or the Teiresias-scene in the *Oedipus Tyrannus* in depth or scope of meaning" (p. 38).

around them."[14] But the point here is that Tiresias, as the play's "prophet," *is* a kind of Sophist or intellectual, who does not draw on his divine inspiration or even his mantic craft, but rather speaks as an intelligent analyst of Dionysus's credentials as a god. His likeness to a Sophist may not make him ridiculous, but it characterizes his wisdom as human rather that divinely inspired.

In his fine oratory, for example, Tiresias describes Dionysus as a god of wine who brings forgetfulness and sleep, a god of prophecy and madness, and one who does not corrupt the chaste women of his rites. As Charles Segal comments, while this may seem quite astute of Tiresias, he "severely misconstrues the nature of Dionysus. Virtually every point he adduces in praise of Dionysus emerges in the subsequent action in just the opposite meaning: nurture of life, release from pain, the Bacchic madness, and so on."[15] In this sense, Tiresias's view of Dionysus and the situation is revealed to be as humanly inadequate as that of Cadmus, who is willing to accept Dionysus's godhood as a convenient fiction, or that of Pentheus, who refuses to accept the god at all. Like most human readers, Tiresias can see only one side of the god, and it is this inability to see or foresee the doubleness or "polysemy" of Dionysus that brings his status as a prophet most under suspicion.

In his speech Tiresias tells a curious story of Dionysus's birth which also diminishes his role as a prophet because he does not acknowledge that there is natural meaning in names and signs. He reacts to critics who say that the story of Dionysus's being saved in Zeus's thigh is improbable by telling a story that is just as silly. The true story, Tiresias says, is that Zeus saved his infant son and modeled out of ether a dummy Dionysus, whom he gave as a hostage (*homēron*) to Hera. Mortals, he

14. Paul Roth, "Teiresias as *Mantis* and Intellectual in Euripides' *Bacchae*," *Transactions of the American Philological Association* 114 (1984): 59–69; quotation on p. 60.

15. Charles Segal, *Dionysiac Poetics and Euripides' "Bacchae"* (Princeton: Princeton University Press, 1982), pp. 295–96.

complains, have mistaken the word *hōmeron* ("hostage") for the word for "thigh" (*to mēros*), imagining that he was put into the thigh (*en mērō*) of Zeus rather than made hostage (*hōmēreuse*) (286–97).

This commentary does more than simply establish the character of Tiresias's rational theology. The appeal to the instability of language represents a peculiar twist on the usual arguments about linguistic nature and convention.[16] Quite the contrary of finding "natural" meaning in words, as it might appear, Tiresias's correction indicates the slipperiness of meaning inherent in conventional signification. He suggests that the words for "hostage" and "thigh" sound quite similar, but they give rise to completely different stories, one supposedly "true" and divine and the other invented by mortals. The account harks back to the misinterpretation in the *Iliad* of divine prodigies that appear "natural," but whose conventional nature is revealed in the fact that they can be misconstrued. Far from ratifying the "true" account of Dionysus's birth, Tiresias's retelling thus suggests the conventional nature of both stories rather than the "natural" quality of the "true" one, as both are linked to the conventional signification of words.

While it may look like the traditional defiance of prophecy, the encounter between Tiresias and Pentheus is undermined by Tiresias's own failure as a prophet. We may conclude that Tiresias has no access to any special or mystic insight here when we see that his "prophecy" of Dionysus does not come true in the play. But Tiresias admits as much in his last words to Pentheus: "I'm not speaking prophecy here: I'm talking about the facts" (*mantikē men ou legō, tois pragmasin de*, 368–69). Like Tiresias when he first appears in *Antigone*, this Tiresias is no more than a counselor, perhaps a little "wandering in the wits," to echo Hector's complaint about Polydamas. But unlike *Antigone*'s Tiresias, this one knows nothing other than "the facts," and he speaks no word that cannot be taken back.[17]

16. See Segal, pp. 294, 296.
17. But cf. R. P. Winnington-Ingram, *Euripides and Dionysus: An Inter-*

These examples suggest that the collapse of the heroic defiance of prophecy in Euripides' plays stems from the diminishing of the prophet as well as the instability of the hero. If prophecy is already devalued into a kind of common discourse of advice, then it is hardly worth defying. Euripides thus accomplishes in these characterizations of Tiresias what Sophocles' heroes attempt to do in attacking Tiresias. In Sophocles' plays the hero is not allowed to debase the prophet completely, as the playwright ultimately protects the mystery and power of the prophet's words. But in Euripides' "Theban" plays, even if Tiresias is somehow "right" in the end, he seems to have little to do with the outcome.[18]

In the *Ion* Euripides' attitude toward prophecy is more controversial, because that play's prophet is no mere man but Apollo himself.[19] While it does not directly echo the characteristic conflict between hero and prophet in Sophocles' Theban plays, *Ion* resembles *Oedipus the King* closely enough to illustrate in broader outlines Euripides' complex response to the heroic encounter with prophecy. In *Ion* and *Oedipus the King* the hero's search for his family and thus for his identity are invested in the pronouncement of oracles. Yet in both plays, too, the social formulation of the hero's identity, including the hero's right to free speech and a place in the *polis*, comes into conflict with the gods' definition of human identity as significant only in terms of people's roles in divine plots. Inevitably,

---

pretation of the "Bacchae" (Cambridge: Cambridge University Press, 1948), on the positive role of Tiresias in the *Bacchae*.

18. It might be argued that in the *Bacchae* Dionysus is a kind of prophet figure, endowed with mysterious power, and thus that Pentheus's conflict with him amounts to a defiance of prophecy. Yet we must remember that even as his power is mysterious, Dionysus's actions are subject to criticism, just as the prophet's power is criticized elsewhere; that is, Dionysus is accused of being motivated by selfishness and anger and of representing interests and values that conflict with those of the city.

19. There is, of course, great critical controversy over the representation of Apollo in this play. For the argument that Apollo is not criticized here, see Anne Pippin Burnett, "Human Resistance and Divine Persuasion in Euripides' *Ion*," *Classical Philology* 57 (1962): 99–103; and F. M. Wasserman, *Transactions of the American Philological Association* 71 (1940): 587–604.

both plays investigate the role of oracle and myth, as the divine and human constructions of a person's story.

Ion, like Oedipus, has a single problem in his otherwise gratifying existence: he does not know who his parents are. Oedipus is driven to find his parents because he wants to know. He does not need to know them to establish his social position or inheritance. He does not care if his birth turns out to be common, for, above all, he considers himself to be the son of Chance or *Tychē* (1080), and so no shame can truly touch him. Oedipus's need to know his parents comes from his obsession with knowing everything. For Ion, however, the situation is different. At first, like Oedipus, he is willing to count a god as a symbolic father (136–40). For as long as he lives in the god's precincts, this is enough, and he does not seek to know more. When Xouthos claims him as a son, however, and reveals his plan to take him home to Athens as heir, the situation is radically transformed. As his father is not a native-born Athenian, the identity of Ion's mother is crucial, because without an Athenian mother, Ion will be both a bastard and an alien's son (589–94). Furthermore, if his mother is a freeborn Athenian, he will inherit through her the right to free speech (*parrēsia*), the right so often called upon and protected in Sophocles' Theban plays. Otherwise, his will be the mouth of a slave (*to ge stoma doulon pepatai kouk' echei parrēsian*, 674–75). The stakes are so high that, unlike Oedipus, Ion hesitates to look for the answer. Afraid that he may discover that his mother was a slave (1380–84), he proceeds only because the god has commanded it.

The *Ion* thus reformulates the associations of political identity, family identity, free speech, and the words of the god as they are set up in *Oedipus the King*. In *Oedipus the King*, Oedipus conceives his political identity as separate from his family identity, because his position as *tyrannos*, given by Chance and gained through his skill, is not inherited. Similarly, his right and dedication to free speech are perceived as something innate and "natural" to his character, rather than gained through his parents. It is, of course, ironic that not only does his discovery of his parentage unseat him from the throne but he finds that indeed he did inherit it. Yet while Oedipus is robbed of his authority to command as *tyrannos*, he is not robbed of "free speech," even as he is sent into exile.[20] Ion, however, is quite aware that political freedom and authority are inextricably connected to his birth and identity. He is no one in Athens and has no voice, except as his birth ensures it.[21]

For both Ion and Oedipus, however, the mystery of their birth, as part of their identity and their right to speech, is tied up with the verification of the god's oracles and the reports or stories of mortals. For Oedipus, his right of free speech is at first threatened by oracular silence; he tries to cover that silence with the sound of human voices, putting testimony and accusation against the oracle. In the end, the play suggests that it is this belief in human testimony that traps him. For Ion, however, the establishment of his political identity lies in the balance of the lies, oracles, myths, and reports that are opened up and analyzed in the play, in which the oracle is subject to rational evaluation and human voices begin to speak in riddles.

All the action of *Ion* takes place before the temple of Apollo's oracle at Delphi, an ever-present reminder of the god's role in the plot. For the audience and the women in the play, the temple's facade hides the sacred place from which the god's words issue forth. Apollo himself is absent throughout the play, but other gods speak in his stead. Hermes, Apollo's sometimes unreliable brother, delivers the prologue, and Athena appears at the end to untie several knots, just as Ion is about to charge into the sanctuary to ask his divine patron whether he has lied. Thus throughout the play Apollo preserves the mask of Delphic silence, although he appears to speak through his messengers. It is up to the others—to Athena, the Pythia, Xouthos, Creusa,

---

20. Cf. *Phoenissae* here, on the loss of *parrēsia*, "freedom of speech," as the exile's greatest punishment (391).

21. One wonders at the end how this problem will be resolved, if Creusa's status as his mother is to be suppressed.

Ion, the Old Man and the Chorus—to interpret, explain, and recount the intentions and words of the hidden god.

Much of the action of the play revolves around the interpretation and questioning of the message the Pythia gives in answer to Xouthos's request for *euteknous chrēsmous* (423–24), an oracle promising children. He is told that the first person he will meet when he leaves the temple will be his son—an astonishingly quick fulfillment of his wish. Ion is quite suspicious at first, sure that this "stranger" is mad when Xouthos embraces him. Xouthos says he will tell him the story (*mythos*, 529) which is the oracle (*chrēstēria*, 532), and Ion finds the *mythos* unbelievable. He wants to know from whom Xouthos got it and wonders what witness he may have to the event. Surely, he says, Xouthos misunderstood a riddle of the god (533). These are all questions one might ask about a remarkable story overheard or reported, but not about an oracle. Indeed, Ion has no reason to believe it except that Xouthos reported that Apollo said it. "How could I be your son?" Ion asks, and Xouthos answers, "Don't ask me—ask the god" (543). Because it is what he wants to hear, Xouthos accepts the word on blind faith, but Ion accepts the oracle only grudgingly.

Ion is not the only one who has trouble with this oracle; it provokes various responses in those concerned. Apollo's words make the Chorus angry because they feel the oracle has cheated Creusa. The oracle does not "please them," and they fear it is a trick (*ou gar me sainei thesphata mē tin' echē[i] dolon*, 685). The Old Man is not willing to say that Apollo has lied, but he finds a rational explanation for the circumstances which implicates Xouthos. The Old Man believes that Xouthos, having had a bastard child by a slave and finding Creusa barren, set up the oracle to manipulate the god to recognize his child. Creusa seems to accept this interpretation, for she never speaks out directly against it or the authority of Apollo's words, even as she blames Apollo for her rape and the abandonment of her child. Thus at first the Chorus, the Old Man, and Creusa all suspect that Xouthos has manipulated the Oracle for his own purposes, and they resolve to kill Ion. It remains at the end for Creusa to give a comparable explanation for the oracle: that Apollo has to give *his* bastard son Ion a father, for political and social purposes, guaranteeing a kind of legitimacy that even a divine father is apparently unable to grant.

Euripides thus emphasizes the political and social uses of oracles in a society concerned with authority and legitimacy. First, the oracle is accepted as authoritative speech that may be used and manipulated, either by Xouthos, as a way of legitimizing a bastard son through an apparently "fortuitous" or providential recognition, or by the god himself, as a way of providing social standing for an illegitimate son. Euripides is also making the more radical suggestion that as part of politics and society, oracles may be subject to the standards of judgment that govern all stories or *mythoi*, especially the standards of believability or probability. They must be believed to be socially efficacious, but why would anyone believe them if they are not likely?

What happens in the open space before Apollo's closed temple is exactly such retelling and questioning of all forms of stories.[22] The Chorus, in the parodos, admires the marvels they have only heard fabled (*ar' hos emaisi mytheuetai*, 196–97). Seeing the images of the myths that are depicted on the temple, they desire to see the sanctuary of Delphi itself, of which they have heard a report (*phatis*, 225). Is it really true, they ask, as they have heard, that the temple houses the center (*omphalos*) of the world (224)? Because they may not enter, only Ion can confirm this report for them, in the same way that only Xouthos can confirm what the Oracle said. When Creusa first hesitantly encounters Ion, he asks her to confirm a story he has heard. Is it true, he asks, as it is told (*hōs memytheutai brotois*, 265), that Erichthonius, her father, was born from the earth?

---

22. See Christian Wolff, "The Design and Myth in Euripides' *Ion*," *Harvard Studies in Classical Philology* 69 (1965): 169–94, on the role of telling and retelling stories in the *Ion*.

And is it true, too, or a false story (*ar' alēthes ē matēn logos*, 275), that he sacrificed his other daughters? Creusa verifies these stories as a member of the family, although she witnessed none of the events.

Thus while all the characters are looking for confirmation of stories of events they cannot or did not see, the stories are being brought into question. But the most important story that is told and questioned is that of Creusa's rape by Apollo and the exposure of the resulting child.[23] First she tells the story to Ion as if it were that of a friend, and then the Chorus briefly recounts it. In her central monody, Creusa finally tells the story as her own firsthand knowledge. Then, once the recognition of mother and son is complete, Creusa repeats it to Ion—who then still cannot believe it. It remains for Athena to confirm the truth of what Creusa says, not as a witness to the event but with the conventional authority of the dea ex machina.

Even as Creusa is the only storyteller with firsthand knowledge of the story she recounts, she is the one most suspected of lying, because her story is unbelievable and difficult to tell. To the other characters her tales seem more like oracular speech than narrative. Responding to the story of the "friend," Ion asks, "Why does this stranger always speak in riddles [*ainissetai*], reviling the god with hidden or disguised words [*logoisin ... kryptoisin*]" (429–30). While he suspected Xouthos of not understanding the god's riddles, here Ion sees Creusa as speaking a kind of secret language of enigmas. Creusa, too, is burdened by her own silence, as the absent god holds his. At first she suppresses her story under the story of the "friend," as well

23. See Wolff, p. 170: "The story of Creusa's unwilling union with Apollo, her secret giving birth, and the child's exposure—in the same cave in which the union takes place (17f.)—is repeated six times. The past is continually kept before us, while each telling of the story, always in a somewhat different mode and context, marks sucessive turns of the plot. For all its surface action, intrigues and violent complications, this plot turns on revelations of the truth about the past, on knowledge and recognitions (recalling, in this respect, the story of another foundling, Oedipus)."

as through veiled references and enigmas (in l. 306, for example, Ion asks if she has ever borne a child, and she replies, "Apollo knows my childlessness"). Only after the revelation of Apollo's oracle to Xouthos does Creusa break her silence. "How should I be silent" [*pōs sigasō*, 859]?" she asks, and with nothing to lose, she declares that she will tell her secret publicly (*karyxō*, 911). Like Antigone and Oedipus before her, Creusa is brought to speak her secret and pain, but the difference here is that her secret is also Apollo's.

Creusa's story and Apollo's oracle are thus drawn closer and closer together, as Apollo's oracle is questioned as if it were a story, while Creusa's story takes on the characteristics of oracular speech. The recognition scene, in which Creusa identifies the tokens in the cradle, the signs or *symbola* of the mother (1386), functions as the interpretation of an oracle, even as it confirms Creusa's story. The cradle itself is represented as a new *mythos* (1340) that has been kept hidden all these years in silence (1341) because the god wished it so (1343-44). But if the cradle is a hidden or mysterious sign that the god has now revealed, the tokens within are also the *symbola* of the mother, and not of the god. Ion enjoins Creusa to be silent as he prepares to open it, but this time she will not be silent; she alone can interpret the signs and tell the *mythos* of the cradle by naming the things hidden within and weaving them together in a narrative. Ion identifies her ability to uncover and name the hidden, to bring them to light, as oracular. These things, he says, are found as an oracle (*thesphath' hōs euriskomen*, 1424).[24]

But do the maternal *symbola* have the power of an oracle? Ion pulls Creusa aside and asks her in secret whether she is manipulating Apollo's oracle to hide the shame of a mortal lover. If not, why did Apollo in effect say that Xouthos is his

---

24. Diggle obelizes this passage, but I accept Gilbert Murray's reading in his earlier edition of vol. 2 of *Euripidis Fabulae* (Oxford: Oxford University Press, 1913).

father? Creusa, master interpreter, says that Apollo meant Ion
as an adoptive son, as a gift, but said nothing of his being a
"natural" son to Xouthos. But for Ion, this is not enough:
"Does the god prophesy truly or falsely [in vain]?" (*ho theos
alēthēs ē matēn manteuetai*, 1537), he asks, echoing the very
words with which he questioned the story of Ericthonius (275).
Is he Xouthos' son or the son of Apollo? For Ion the idea that
the word "son" is polysemous, that it can be understood in
both its natural and conventional meanings, is unacceptable;
for him, the truth is absolute, and it must be one or the other.
But when he goes to question the god, Athena imposes the
duality, insisting that *Creusa's* interpretation is right, that
Apollo meant "son" in a legal or conventional rather than a
natural sense, while Apollo is his "biological" father.

The role of Creusa's story and her own function as storyteller
and interpreter are thus extremely complex. At first it appears
that her story is pitted against Apollo's oracle to Xouthos, for
they are contradictory versions of human events. This contradiction can be seen as a recapitulation of the conflict we see in
Oedipus the King between Tiresias's version of the murder of
Laius and Oedipus's story of the conspiracy. Just as Oedipus
represents Tiresias's story as covering up for Creon's murder
of Laius, to Ion the authority of Creusa's tale is suspect, for it
may be just the story of a woman who, to hide her shame over
an illegitimate birth, says that she lay with a god.[25] Yet in her
initial desire to suppress the whole truth, Creusa uses the riddling form of oracular speech, and at the play's end she moves
fully into the role of prophet as she reveals and names what is
hidden in the cradle—her own signs, the *symbola* of the mother
(recalling Clytemnestra's *symbolon* of the beacon fires). Even
as she is cast into the role of the interpreter of her own signs,
however, she is appropriated by Apollo as *his* prophet. Creusa
is the one who links her own and Apollo's "oracles," or stories,

25. Cf. Dionysus's account of the accusations against Semele in the *Bacchae*, ll. 25–32.

of Ion's parentage, by employing the classic methods of oracular apologetics, unfolding the polysemy of the conventional sign of "son." It could be said that in the end she becomes a prophet in her own right, but only to serve the god who violated her. This reconciliation is quite different from that between the human voice and divine sign which Sophocles brings about in the later *Oedipus at Colonus.* There Oedipus does not so much serve Apollo as become like a god himself. Creusa, however, is more like Tiresias, the mortal who mediates between the words of the gods and human language and understanding.

That Athena's speech is needed at the end to ratify Creusa's story and defend Apollo's role in prophesying to Xouthos points to the fragility of the kind of compromise between divine oracle and human story which Creusa's acceptance and speaking represent. While Athena comes to speak in her person, Apollo does not, lest he be blamed for the rape. Sending a substitute, he remains hidden. Athena explains that matters got a little out of hand: Apollo had intended, as Hermes said in the prologue, that Creusa should recognize Ion later in Athens, but his true family was revealed now to avert disaster. She prophesies that future generations of Ion's descent shall populate Asia and Europe and be called Ionians. Finally, Athena calls for silence, insisting that Xouthos must continue to believe that Ion is his son, to ensure his place in the city.

Athena's speech thus attempts to reforge the strained links between oracle and story. On the one hand, the oracle is subject to rational interpretation and practical justification, as it represents Apollo's *mēchanē* or "plot" (1565), which counteracts the *mēchanē* of Creusa and the Old Man to kill Ion (1116). On the other hand, the oracle is still mysterious, having its origin in an absent and hidden god, just as Creusa's story in the end, like the grave of Oedipus in Colonus, must never be revealed in Athens, but must be protected by silence. The oracle and story both, once verified, must be remystified to ensure their power. Athena's focus here is on closure, the provision of a happy ending to near disaster which is one function of oracles. As Athena says, the gods may take some time to act, but they are not weak in the end (*es telos*, 1615)—or endings. This emphasis on the importance of the conclusion is reflected in the last lines, which claim that in the end (*es telos*) good men turn out well, and the bad are punished (1621–22). The *telos* of the *Ion* itself has been achieved with an awareness of the investment of the gods' authority in *telē*, as well as of the moral significance of endings. What is crucial in the gods' ability to bring about endings is, as Ion suggests, the matter of belief. As in *Oedipus the King*, the hero must be the one, finally, to accept the god's versions of events. In Sophocles' play, for everyone to believe Oedipus's guilt, Oedipus himself must say it is true. In the *Ion*, the young man, too, ultimately accepts the divine word: "We have received your words," Ion says to Athena, "without disbelief [*ouk apistia*(i)]; I believe that Apollo and she are my parents—and before it was not unbelievable [*ouk apiston*]" (1606–8). Yet, unlike the case in *Oedipus the King*, here Euripides characteristically formulates Ion's belief in terms of the negation of disbelief, just as he suggests that the tale's "believability" has been overdetermined, with Athena's words supplementing Creusa's. The playwright reminds us that the story does not have its effect and the gods do not function without belief; and without belief, there is no end of irony.

The *Ion* opens with a lyrical image of destruction which delicately articulates the play's incomplete erasure of the sacred meaning invested in signs. As Apollo's servant, Ion must keep the god's temple clean. He sweeps the floor with laurel and sprinklings of water and kills the birds who would foul the temple, aiming his bow at the eagle, the messenger of Zeus (158–59), and at the swan, the clear-voiced singer. What has happened here to those terrifying "winged words," the *oiōnoi* of Homer, who swept down on the armies to bear the gods' stern messages? Worse than the birds of *Antigone*, who desecrate the Theban altars with scraps of dead flesh, these eagles and swans are common birds, and very real birds, who leave no mark or message other than the stains of their dung. It makes Ion a bit uneasy, all the same, to kill the birds who foul the shrine, because he *does* recognize them as messengers who bear the oracles of gods (*phēmas*) to mortals (180–81). Thus while Euripides does have Ion accept the birds as significant, he also has Ion kill them to honor the god who has nurtured him. They are *oiōnoi* killed in the service of the god of prophecy, to purify the place of the god who, in Heraclitus's formula, only "signifies." In the same way, Euripides has everything significant—love, belief, truth—here attacked and then appropriated to maintain and glorify Apollo's sanctuary, wreathed with the silent images of the fabled gods. Delphi still stands, in the end, closed and blank except for those images of our myths painted on it.

Index

Library of Congress Cataloging-in-Publication Data

Bushnell, Rebecca W., 1952–
    Prophesying tragedy.

    Bibliography: p.
    Includes index.
    1. Sophocles. Oedipus Rex. 2. Sophocles. Oedipus
at Colonus. 3. Sophocles. Antigone. 4. Oedipus
(Greek mythology) in literature. 5. Antigone
(Legendary character) in literature. 6. Thebes (Greece)
in literature. 7. Tragic, The, in literature.
8. Prophecies in literature. I. Title.
PA4413.07B87 1988   882'.01   87–47857
ISBN 0-8014-2132-2 (alk. paper)